SIFTING THROUGH IDALIA'S PAST

Written by the Idalia Writing Lab

Gusts of Dust III

Written by
The 2001-2002 Writing Lab
Idalia High School
Idalia, Colorado

Edited with an Introduction
by Lucille Rossbach,
Teacher implementing
the Foxfire Approach

Published by Dennis Schiel, Artist

Vol. III

Gusts of Dust III
SIFTING THROUGH IDALIA'S PAST
Volume III

ISBN 0-9658072-4-X

Copyright © 2002 by Lucille Rossbach and/or Dennis Schiel
Written by Idalia High School 2001-2002 Writing Lab Students
Edited by Lucille Rossbach, teacher implementing the Foxfire Approach
Published by Dennis Schiel, Artist
P.O. Box 57
Idalia, CO 80735

Printed in the United States of America

Contents

Dedication

We offer this volume of <u>Gusts of Dust</u>

in honor of the men and women

who gave their service to our country

in defense of freedom.

We salute you!

Memorial

We remember with gratitude
the men who freely shared stories
from their life
for the recorded history of our
community:
Charlie Brenner
James Hutton
John McCoy
Punk North

Introduction

By
Lucille Rossbach

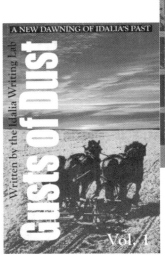

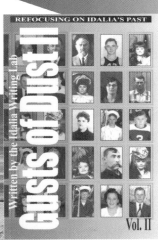

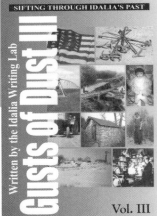

Two eighteen-foot, white limos slid in front of the Tattered Cover Book Store in Denver, and tuxedoed drivers hustled around to stiffly open rear passenger doors, not for a local celebrity stopping for a quick purchase or some distinguished authors just flown in for book signings, but instead for a handful of small-town teenagers neatly groomed but nervously trying to hide their giddiness. "We've had teachers in here signing their books," said Samantha Bennett, special events coordinator of the Tattered Cover, "but we've never had students. This is a first."

What precipitated that special invitation to Idalia students from such a renowned book store? These students, members of the Writing Lab class, had written the first two volumes of *Gusts of Dust*, putting into print previously unpublished, oral histories of their neighbors and also once again recording information that is now out-of-print. And that experience inspired us to do a third volume. But why do Idalians preorder copies before the book goes to our publisher? Why was Volume II nominated for a Colorado Book of the Year Award? Why have professional authors, professors unknown to our students, and Idalia citizens written to the Writing Lab students to say "good job"? What is the appeal of *Gusts of Dust*?

June Redman, volunteer archivist at the Wray Museum, most succinctly and accurately summarizes the value of these books by saying, "This period is culture, and things are changing so fast...if we don't record it, it will be lost." Yes, it is crucial that Brooklynn records how the old party-line telephones used to work, that Kendra documents how Idalians reflected the fashions of the 1920's, that Molly tells of what could be found in the old general stores, or that Jobediah describes how sod provided homes for our settlers.

And as teacher of the Writing Lab class, I am often tempted to assign topics that the students should research. Instead, I insist that they choose and write about the topics that interest them. At times I try to influence their choices because I believe something needs to be recorded NOW, but essentially students choose to write on anything that has some connection with Idalia's history. I truly believe if I assigned topics, they would tire and bulk at the tremendous task before them. If they choose the topics, their research has more depth and their interest doesn't wane, making them more willing to check and recheck, and then recheck once more, the information they record as history.

But as the students record the information they gather, they also document our unique culture, our farming and ranching life. When one realizes that only a very small percentage of Americans are stewarts of America's farmland and that we are sitting on a shrinking aquifer, Whitney's stories about harvesting wheat and German's history of irrigation in this area take on renewed meaning. But Idalia not only contributes to our nation's bread basket, we also help supply meat for America's tables. Therefore, a consideration of Idalia's culture would not be complete without Cowboy Colt's details on branding or Brooklyn's research of the ranch on which she lives.

But something else happens as these students record our history and culture. Much like the oral histories of ancient civilizations, passed down from one generation to the next until someone eventually puts the stories into written format, the oral histories of Idalia reinforce the values of our community. Each of these now recorded stories reflect our values of working hard, helping our neighbors, and setting goals to achieve dreams. They also emphasize the importance of family values, dignity and kindness, and a good education. And more poignantly, as evidenced by the stories Ryan gathered on the 1935 Flood, we hold a God-fearing respect for nature and the belief that good comes out of suffering. Above all, we're humbly appreciative of the sacrifices others made for us and our nation; therefore, Candice chose to honor all our hometown veterans by including some of their stories.

September 11, 2001, horrifically impacted all of us. The attack on that shattering day led us to re-examine our lives, reprioritize our values, and return to our basic beliefs. But the community of Idalia had started that process several years earlier. Neil's stories about the ghost towns of Yuma County make us realize how easily Idalia could have become one more of those demised communities. Just a very few years ago, the "talk" around our community was that "Wray wanted to close the Idalia School" because it had become a "financial burden" to the East Yuma County RJ-2 School District. But Idalians responded to that possibility by building a new gymnasium, the biggest gymnasium east of Denver, the biggest gymnasium on the entire Eastern High Plains of Colorado. And then we deconsolidated from the larger Wray schools. In essence, we said, "We will not go away!"

But more than our school had been threatened. Because our school is the gathering place of the community, we would not just have lost our school; we would also have lost our sense of community and our unique culture. *Gusts of Dust* records the voices of those who refused to let our community die, the voices that reflect our indomitable human spirit. Their stories exemplify the power and value of individuals in small places. They say, "Our lives matter!"

And, ultimately, that's it! We DO need to know that our lives matter! Yes, we have a hunger to know our heritage. But we also strive to leave a mark and to inspire future generations. And when we are about to die, we want assurance that our lives had meaning, that we have not lived in vain. The recorded narratives in *Gusts of Dust* do all of that. They tell us who we are and where we come from, but they also shed light for those coming after us

Often the elderly in our society are made to feel as if they have little to offer, but the *Gusts of Dust* writers say otherwise. During work on our first volume, as many of our elderly citizens came to realize that our young people really do want to hear their stories, they started to come during or after school to drop off artifacts and old photos. They still do that and willingly give interviews, arranging their schedules to accommodate student schedules. They know their lives matter. And their reality becomes our reality, so we grieve when they die, remembering the beautiful stories they shared with us~now recorded for posterity. Thank you, John McCoy, for recognizing the contributions of *Gusts of Dust* in your obituary. We are honored by your continued influence via your recorded stories.

Stories truly do bind people together; they bridge the generations; they shape and define us. Increasingly, I am convinced that learning is a social activity; and as we visit with friends, stories serve as forms of pleasure and entertainment, but they also become powerful ways to learn about ourselves and others. The stories of Idalia's "Homer," Clarence Lidke, alone would fill an entire volume of *Gusts of Dust*; and he has that special gift of always entertaining and instructing via his stories. But usually, "stories" are not thought of as "literature." Ironically, though, a most common definition for literature is "writing that instructs and entertains."

I know that the *Gusts of Dust* writers clearly see themselves as recorders of history, but I'm not sure they ever consider themselves to be creators of literature. The Colorado Department of Education "got it right" when they formulated Standards for Reading and Writing. Standard Six calls for students to "read and recognize literature as a record of human experience." Isn't that exactly what the volumes of *Gusts of Dust* do? Don't they provide a record of human experiences? In fact, literature and writing textbooks have always recognized the power of stories; they just refer to them as "narratives" or "biographies" rather than mundane "stories."

Stories truly do instruct, but they must also please. A poorly-written story or a poorly-told experience is not pleasing, is not "literature." Just as petroglyphs on rocks contextualized history, so have these high schoolers given meaning with the stories they recorded. But perhaps the primary purpose of the petroglyphs was not just to instruct, to record history; perhaps they originated with artists at work. Clearly, our community values both the stories that get recorded and the artistry of the writing.

Chuck Brandon, former Idalia resident, in a letter dated December 31, 2001, writes, "You are to be congratulated and commended in utilizing this approach for educating the students of Idalia School in the history and benefits of their community as well as appropriate construction and usage of the English language." And June Redman, at the Wray Museum (which currently houses much of Idalia's archival information), when asked about the value of *Gusts of Dust*, immediately said, "It gives students creative writing experience." And the students have written creatively! Woven among the stories, one finds memoirs, anecdotes, dialogues, folk tales, tall tales, narrative structures, vivid imagery, poetry, drama, and essays.

Clearly, we need to consider doing another volume of *Gusts of Dust* some day. So much more history still needs to be recorded. But we also need to have a generous citizen donate a building to start our own museum, bring home our documents from the Wray Museum, and add to them. We need to gather artifacts such as a burlap-wrapped vinegar jug taken to harvesters at mid-day, a 1920's dress worn on a float during Idalia's Centennial celebration, pillow covers brought home by our veterans, audio tapes and videos of recorded interviews with our citizens, photos presently lying in file drawers and on shelves at Idalia School and in many people's homes, and hopefully another volume of *Gusts of Dust*. One hundred years from now, these books will be important ethnographical documents!

Lucille Rossbach
Teacher implementing the Foxfire Approach

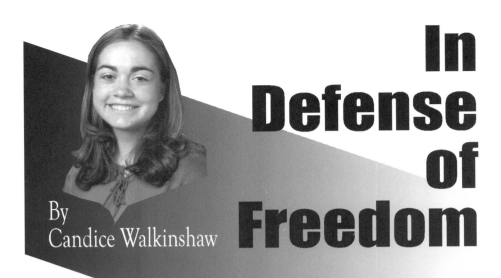

In Defense of Freedom

By
Candice Walkinshaw

The American flag during World War II only contained forty-eight stars. Writing Lab photos of artifacts supplied by Lucy Eastin.

The Honolulu Star Bulletin issued December 7, 1941, states that "President Roosevelt announced this morning that Japanese planes had attacked Manila and Pearl Harbor." Writing Lab photo taken at Wray Museum

America's veterans have always created a valuable history of the United States. But now, more than ever, we look to our military forces for courage and guidance. We fight the same battle today that they fought years ago. The veterans of the past fought for and gained freedom and the level of respect that America currently has. Because people tried to penetrate America in the bombing of the World Trade Center, our troops again have to go on to foreign soil to gain back that respect for freedom. The reason I chose this topic is because of the courage that the current troops and the veterans of the past have shown. It is so remarkable to me, and I want to do my part in honoring them, however little it may be compared to what they truly deserve. To honor all our veterans and current troops, our Writing Lab class chose to place this story at the beginning of this book, which is dedicated to them.

Idalia has been proud to be part of America and has guided the younger generations in sharing their patriotism toward our flag. Many of the older residents of the Idalia community have fought in one war or another. A few of those veterans whom I was able to interview include Alvin Langendoerfer, Clarence Lidke, and Frank Walters of World War II; and Jim Schiel and Junior Weisshaar of the Korean War.

Idalia Veterans of World War II from whom I was unable to get a story, but who still served for America, include Corporal Howard Armkneckht, reported missing while in Italy but was later found safe; Franz John Brenner, killed in action March 3, 1945, while in Northern Italy and awarded the Gold Star; Coast Guardsman Raymond Brinkhoff, honored for aiding 265 wounded men aboard ship while the enemy fired on them; Raymond R. Busby, RT 3/C, assigned on the USS Herin; Staff Sergeant Mervin Busby, stationed at a B-29 base in Calcutta, India; Sergeant J.W. Clark, received the Bronze Star for an act of heroism in Germany; Dalton Lee Cody, reported under the casualty listing of the February 1944 *Our Navy* magazine as "missing in action"; Sergeant Fred L. Crites, served in

England with the Army Air Force; Helmut Dietrich, an Idalia minister's son killed at Pearl Harbor on December 7, 1941, and awarded the Gold Star; Harry E. Ekberg, volunteered for the Navy and repaired battle wagons; Eldon M. Elliot, technical sergeant killed in action on October 25, 1942, in the Pacific and awarded the Gold Star; Colonel James D. Garcia, received an air medal, killed in a B-29 accident on Guam and awarded the Gold Star; Sergeant Charles F. Jordan, decorated with the Distinguished Flying Cross during flights in the Southwest Pacific; Sergeant Everett Miller, received technical training at the Army Postal School in Westchester, Pennsylvania, and served with the American Army in France; Delbert Morris, RM 3/C, stationed in the South Pacific doing transport duty; Lieutenant William Morris, shot down at Pearl Harbor but survived unharmed; Captain Gilbert Ostrander, awarded the Bronze Star for heroic action in the Italian Campaign; Johnny B. Terry, S 2/C, and Corporal T/5 William C. Terry, brothers who served in the Philippines.

Not all of these men were from Idalia originally, but they found their roots here at one time or another and were featured in the *Idalia Centennial 1887-1987* and *The Gold Star Boys*. Gold Stars honor men and women killed in United States military combat.

World War I

WWI was the first major war that truly affected Idalia residents; however, I wasn't able to get much information on Idalians in WWI. Most of the people that would remember it have already died, but the hardships of WWI did affect the Idalia community, affecting emotions more than anything. The majority of Idalia citizens were of German descent; so having their home country in war with their newfound home really struck them close to their hearts. At the time many families went from speaking German to strictly English in order to prove their loyalty to America. (*Idalia Centennial*, p. 5)

Helmets such as this provided protection for British soldiers during World War II. Great Britain and the United States served as two of the allied forces in the fight against Nazism. Writing Lab photo taken at Wray Museum.

World War II

Wars affect many more people than just the soldiers who fight in them. This was especially the case during WWII. Young men who were not drafted went to California to build airplanes and ships. The whole country came together to contribute time and money. Even ordinary towns as small as Idalia were affected and felt the blow of this war as their young men left to serve our country. WWII lasted from 1939-1945. The United States entered the war after Japan bombed Pearl Harbor on December 7, 1941. It's been called the most destructive war known because more than seventeen million people died, and the war left many countries on the brink of collapse ("Guts and Glory"). Alvin Langendoerfer, Clarence Lidke, and Frank Walters are three local men who served in that war.

Alvin Langendoerfer, who now lives in Burlington, Colorado, is a Veteran of WWII, drafted in July of 1942 and discharged in February of 1946. He started out as a Personnel

Alvin Langendoerfer of Burlington, Colorado, veteran of World War II, served from July 1942 to February 1946. Photo courtesy of Alvin Langendoerfer.

Clerk and stayed in that position for about two years. "I was then a Private First Class, which means I was exempt from most of the KP and guard duty and stuff like that," said Alvin. He went to the European theatre in December of 1944, and from there his destination was to be the Battle of the Bulge, which is said to be the bloodiest battle of WWII, with nearly 80,000 Americans killed, wounded, or captured ("Guts and Glory"). "We were sent over in an armada with about seventy vessels of all sizes; and on the way over, there were fighter planes going over us making sure we weren't being attacked. We had several threats, though, and we never knew which ones were real," he said. When they landed in England on December 22, they had a two- to three-week delay. Then finally they discovered that their guns, the 155 Long Tom Artillery, have been sunk on the way over; and they didn't know where they were to go from there. "We were then delayed for another month while we got new equipment. By that time the Battle of the Bulge was over."

They then went from England to France and were delayed approximately a week under strict camouflage, while waiting for the next assignment: crossing the Rhine. "Camouflaging thirty-five vehicles and four pieces of heavy artillery was nearly impossible, but somehow we were able to cover everybody so that we weren't visible from the air. And for three days nobody could go out," Alvin said. "For about three days before we crossed the Rhine, it was almost a constant string of airplanes, pulling gliders and flying near by, and somewhere in the neighborhood of fifteen to twenty thousand troops jumping out of those." They finally crossed the Rhine on a bridge made of pontoons. They crossed in trucks that pulled artillery.

While Alvin was in World War II, he fought in seven major battles. He said, "From the time we entered the war until it was over, why you couldn't tell one battle from the other. It was one continuous mess."

At one time he was within a mile of where General Patton was killed. He and everyone else were very disappointed in the information, or lack of information, they received. The paper called *Stars*

Men and women in military service often brought home souvenirs from where they were stationed for their family members. While serving during World War II, Eugene Collins bought pillow covers for his mother Lois Collins, then of Wray, Colorado. He purchased the above covers from Wendover Field, Utah; San Antonio, Texas; and England. The bottom two contain "Mother" poems. Writing Lab photos of artifacts supplied by Lucy Eastin.

and Stripes issued to all soldiers never once mentioned what happened to General Patton's driver or the people who killed him. General Patton was said to be one of the ablest U.S. commanders in World War II. The PBS website quoted him as saying, "Compared to war, all other forms of human endeavor shrink to insignificance" ("Guts and Glory"). Reportedly, General Patton died in a jeep accident.

Clarence Lidke, Idalia, Colorado, graduated from the Army Air Force Gunnery School in Texas. He flew thirty-five missions over Nazi Germany as a Ball Gunner on a B-24 while serving with the

446th Heavy Bomb Group. He says, "I never fired my guns for business because the B-51s did an excellent job of keeping the FW190s and ME109s out of our hair." He received a Ssgt. Air Medal, but he much too humbly qualifies that by saying, "Most ground force personnel were part of a larger group under one officer in command, so the officer may have only known that someone stuck his neck out a long ways to get in position to take out a machine gun position, or something on that order, without knowing which of his men did the job. So the man never got recognition. With us in Air Crews, our C.O. personally knew us all and usually knew exactly what each of us was doing, so we could have received recognition often for doing something much less dangerous, often just for doing what we were trained to do and no more."

Clarence also tells about some of the prisoners of war that were located around Vernon. He said, "The Italians were reluctant about fighting us, so we would capture them and bring them to the middle of nowhere to help in the war effort." They would stay with individual farmers and help the farmers with chores and any other happenings on the farm. "There weren't many prisoners who tried to escape," he said. "They were better off working and getting fed than having to fight us."

Frank Walters, now of Burlington, Colorado, also fought in

Ration Stamps, issued during World War II, allowed people to purchase essential but limited items. Stamps helped purchase this pair of wooden-soled shoes, marketed instead of regular shoes because of the rubber shortage during the war. Writing Lab photos of artifacts supplied by Lucy Eastin.

WWII. He ascended basic training in California and was shipped without leave to the Pacific. He then served in New Guinea. While there he "contracted malaria...was sent back to Sydney, Australia, to hospital...and after convalescing was entered into a motor pool and Hdq. Co." After thirty-three months overseas, he was sent back to the United States and stationed in Missouri until he was discharged on September 30, 1945.

A Unique Concentration Camp Story

At the end of WWII the United States sent troops into Europe to clean up the concentration camps the Nazis had used. Dustin Cloyd, senior at Idalia High School, tells a story told to him by Harold Cloyd, his grandfather who lives in Nampa, Idaho. Harold was with

Eugene Collins (1921-1997), brother of Lucy Eastin of Eckley, Colorado, and son of the late Irvine and Lois Collins, Wray, Colorado, served as Private First Class in the Army Air Corp during World War II. After doing basic training at Sheppard Field in Texas, he shipped to Wendover Air Base in Utah and then on to England. Men and women away at war would correspond frequently through letters. But before letters reached their destination, they were screened and censored of any information about the war and the writer's exact location. Writing Lab photos of artifacts supplied by Lucy Eastin.

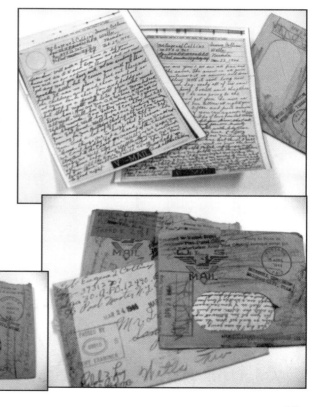

one of those troops who was on clean-up duty for the camps, and one day he told the following story "out of the blue, after keeping it hidden from me for so long," said Dustin. What follows is the unbelievable story that Dustin relates, a story many people have yet to hear.

"At the end of the war, he (Harold) was on the clean-up crew for one of the concentration camps for the Jews. He hadn't seen much because he arrived about the time the war ended. As he walked through the camp, he thought of what occurred on the very ground where he was standing. It almost made him sick. All of the people had died for useless reasons; one man's hatred had killed millions of people. He then went to see the commanding officer to get orders for duty. As he was walking to his destination, he saw a group of Jewish prisoners, one of them talking very calmly to the officer and troop around them; the other man there was a German officer...with a noose around his neck. He was about to be hung.

"Grandpa said that the German officer was very composed, with nothing but a few tears rolling down his cheek. Grandpa then saw a close friend in the troop, who stood around listening to the prisoners talk; so Grandpa went on his way to get orders, figuring on getting the story from his friend later. He carried out his orders but kept thinking back to the man with a noose around his neck and what the Jewish prisoners might have been saying. Finally his curiosity overcame him, and he asked his friend about it."

"He told me this," said Grandpa to Dustin. "The Jewish prisoners were pleading for the German's life because he had been good to them; he fed them more than only what was needed to survive, and he was a fair man. They pleaded for the man's life because he had been fair to them. That he was responsible for killing many of them in gas chambers and such they already knew, but they were pleading for his life like he was one of their own." Grandpa said, "The Americans had no choice in the matter but to hang the German for his offenses in the war; but the thing is, the prisoners got down on their knees and prayed for this officer, this man who had killed their own people. They got down and prayed."

This story is truly remarkable. One always hears of how tortured and weak the Jewish prisoners were, and I know they were. But despite all their despair, they were able to fight for another man's life after they themselves had faced death.

Korean War

The next major war that affected the United States was the Korean War and, like in all the other wars, men from Idalia participated in the battles. Two such men are Jim Schiel and Junior Weisshaar.

Jim Schiel, Idalia, Colorado, fought in the Korean War. He was inducted on June 15, 1951, and discharged on March 14, 1953. Then he went into the Army Reserve on March 15, the following day, and was discharged from the U.S. Army in October of 1956. He spent his sixteen weeks of basic training in Arkansas "where I was trained for everything you would possibly need to know in war." He then went overseas to Japan on a merchant ship. From there he went to medical school for thirty days to become a line medical aidman, which put him on the front line for almost ten months before he was transferred out and sent home when his tour was finished.

Junior Weisshaar, Idalia, Colorado, also fought in the Korean War. He started his training in November of 1952. After eight weeks of basic training, he had eight weeks of heavy weapon training. On the ship to Korea, he celebrated his twenty-first birthday. Junior said, "When I wasn't on the line, I was in a police action duty." He was in Korea when the war ended.

Since the Korean War, others from Idalia have served in foreign conflict, especially Vietnam and the Gulf War; however, I didn't gather these stories because I wanted to focus my efforts on recording some stories of our older veterans.

Every war presents acts of heroism, but different acts of bravery and a "new type of war" have just started. It's the War on Terrorism, and America is on the defense, fighting back all the hatred and rage directed our way. We're also using this War, something evil, as a lesson for our youth. We know that even when things go wrong, the best medicine is still love and forgiveness.

Some Idalia students took a role in passively fighting the Taliban and Al Queda by participating in a nation-wide program which invited school children in the United States to give one dollar each to provide food for Afghanistan's starving children. We are building a strong future to fortress our strong past, but who would have guessed that we could use our own generosity as a "weapon" against evil?

Military uniforms indicate rank and specific branches of military service. The "wings" on a WWII Army Air Force uniform indicate the rank of Second Lieutenant.

A member of the Army Medical Corps wore this uniform during the same war. Each stripe on the sleeve represents three years of service.

"Battle Dress" for men in the field during WWII included this United States Army Staff Sergeant's jacket, trousers, top coat, and hat.

During WWII, a Private First Class of the US Marine Corps used this dress jacket.

Writing Lab photos taken at Wray Museum.

The Call To Serve

While looking through old newspaper articles at the Wray Museum, I found the following poem and wished to present it here in honor of all war veterans. We were fortunate enough to contact the poet, Al Renzelman of Sterling, Colorado. Al is known to many Idalia residents because of his work through the Northeastern Board of Centralized Education Services, and he gave his consent for us to publish his poem. "I wrote it at a time when they (Bud Wells and others) were asking for pictures and short stories from those who served in World War II," Al said regarding the reasons for writing the poem. He also said, "I write from the heart as I'm inspired to do so," which is evident in this poem.

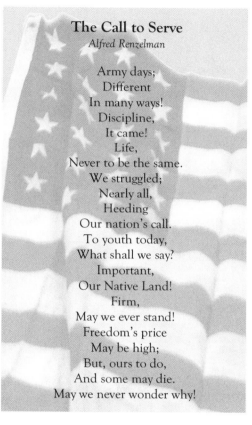

The Call to Serve
Alfred Renzelman

Army days;
Different
In many ways!
Discipline,
It came!
Life,
Never to be the same.
We struggled;
Nearly all,
Heeding
Our nation's call.
To youth today,
What shall we say?
Important,
Our Native Land!
Firm,
May we ever stand!
Freedom's price
May be high;
But, ours to do,
And some may die.
May we never wonder why!

Sources:
Dustin Cloyd, Idalia, Colorado
Lucy Eastin, Eckley, Colorado
Clarence Lidke, Idalia, Colorado
David C. Rossbach, St. Francis, Kansas
James Schiel, Idalia, Colorado
Frank Walters, Burlington, Colorado
Junior Weisshaar, Idalia, Colorado
Brandon, Chuck. Letter. *Wray Gazette*. Wray, Colorado, 1998.
Gold Star Boys. Scrapbook of World War II Soldiers who died in action, compiled by
    Stephen Chaplain and presented by the Yuma Museum to the Wray Museum.
"Guts and Glory." http://www.pbs.org/wgbh/amex/guts/indes.html
Idalia Centennial 1887-1987
Wells, Bud, ed. *World War II and the People of Yuma County*. Dallas, Texas: Curtis Media
    Corporation, 1993.
Wray Museum

Old Town Window Dreams

By
Molly Manser

A roll of linoleum and a lone telephone stand amid the jumble of the Yount Store in 1921. The store served the Vernon, Colorado, area from 1914 to 1922 in the Stevens Building selling General Merchandise.
Photo courtesy of Wray Museum.

As a third-year Writing Lab student, I thought this year's Writing Lab class would be a breeze. I had thought that I had done it all and would not struggle this year due to my "experience." That proved false! Even with my "three years of experience," each year prior presented new challenges. This year was no exception. Every year there are more people to interview, other research to dig up, and new stories to write and present in a factual and creative way. And I am still amazed at how much work goes into creating a <u>Gusts of Dust</u> book. But I will honestly say it is worth it. As a senior this is my last year in Writing Lab, but I will take the skills that I have learned with me into life.

I would like to thank everyone who has purchased a copy or copies of a <u>Gusts of Dust</u> book. Without your support it would never have been possible to take the Writing Lab dream as far as we did. Thank you. I would also like to thank the interviewees. Without you there would be no stories and there would be no books. Thank you. And I would like to thank Mrs. Rossbach. She has been the heart and soul of the Writing Lab class and, through her inspiration and creative thinking, put together a class that is unlike any other writing class presented at a high school level. Thank you.

Walking down the red brick road, I veer left and stop upon reaching my destination. The immaculately kept, white building stands out from the other buildings due to its facade, a false front added to make the building have a taller appearance. I push my way inside, through the heavy wooden doors, and I stop to survey the room. Glossed to a high shine, a long wooden counter prominently stands to the right. Behind this counter, a wall of shelves hangs from ceiling to floor. Carefully placed tins, bottles, and numerous little packages lie silently waiting along the shelves. As I glance to the left, I notice three, large, wooden barrels standing near the back. I chuckle to myself, remembering a story a wise woman had told me about how they "stored all kinds of goods in those barrels." Looking further to the left, I notice more wall-to-wall shelves packed tightly with more items. Turning back to face the door, I realize I have over-looked a small post office quietly standing in the corner. Directly across from it sits a butcher's block. Then glancing down at my wristwatch, I gasp as I take notice of the time.

Hurriedly I prop open the front doors and arrange my bowl of peanut brittle and suckers which will be distributed throughout the day. I rehearse my speech one last time and put a smile on my face as the first children bound through the welcoming front doors.

"Hello," I say, "my name is Molly, and I will be your Old Town General Store tour guide for the day." As I look over the youngsters' faces, my mind wanders back to the morning's events. . .

It was my first day on the job at Old Town, in Burlington, Colorado. Old Town is a magical place where creative individuals recreated an "Old Town" complete with buildings and artifacts. I would be working there all summer as a Can-Can Girl, but for my first day's assignment I would be the General Store's tour guide. That day happened to be the annual "School Days," a one-day event when bus-loads of children come from around the state to spend an educational and fun-filled day at Old Town. While there they get to tour the old buildings, sit in on the Can-Can Show in the Longhorn Saloon, and dine on sodas and sundaes in the Soda Fountain.

When I arrived at work that morning, I had no idea what was awaiting me for my day's workload. Then another new girl and I were told that we would be tour guides, and we had our choice between the General Store and the sod house. My sister had worked at Old Town for a few years prior to my job there, and I had previously visited her and been inside the sod house. I didn't remember much about it, but I remembered that it was very dark, so I chose the General Store to avoid having a dreary day. I then received a sheet of historical facts on my building and headed for the store. As I read through my sheet, I learned a gigantic history lesson. I committed those facts to memory for what I thought would be used only during tour guiding, but now a year later I still remember those facts held by that paper.

While choosing an article topic at the beginning of this school

Green grapes lazily lean against a cash register, advertising scrumptious Nut Tootsie Rolls, in the Wray Museum. Writing Lab photo.

Basking in the sun at the Wray Museum, these oranges, apples, pears, and grapefruit appear as if they are waiting to be bagged and purchased. Writing Lab photo.

year, I remembered back to my summer at Old Town and thought fondly of the General Store there. I knew at that point that my main article would focus on general store information, especially since Old Idalia had once had a general store on its main street. Later in the year our class visited the Wray Museum, and I was delighted to see that they opened a room filled with general store artifacts. June Redman, one of Wray Museum's volunteer curators and an avid member of our community, was excited to hear that I was doing a story on general stores and she bubbled with information on them.

"General stores were the carry-all stores," said June, "where farmers would come to barter and buy pretty much anything that they needed. When you review history, you will see sometimes there were towns that had only a general store. The towns eventually died out, but they were needed at the time for it was necessary to have many general stores around. It would take families a whole day to venture the ten or fifteen-mile journey it took to get to the nearest general store. When you approached the general store, you would notice that it was usually a one or two-story building with large display windows in the front."

In addition, general stores usually had the well-known facades. Later when main streets were built into the towns, many other buildings, even saloons, adopted the facade appearances.

June continued, "When you walked inside, shelves upon shelves met you. And wooden counters stretched along the sides of the store. The shelves usually had drawers built into them that held flour, coffee, sugar, and other dried products. Behind the counters, the shelves were stocked with common household items such as medicines, spices, and baking materials. General stores sold everything and anything. They had produce, grocery items, clothing, tools, and farming equipment. And if they didn't have something that you needed, you could order it through the storekeeper, and he would pick it up on his next visit into the city."

To accommodate small town life, Peggy Carpenter still does this today in order to run her little Idalia store, Carpenter's Mini-Mall. She often ventures to Burlington or Wray to pick up goods for area shoppers.

"Since they didn't have grocery bags, everything was packaged in brown paper and tied up with string," added June. "There is an old story about how the ice cream cone was invented. They say that goes

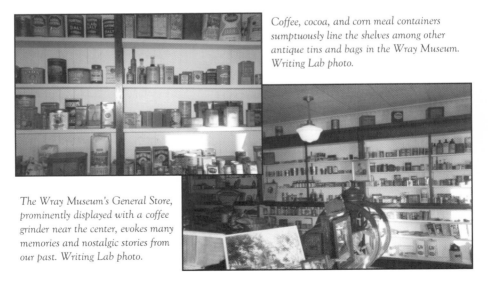

Coffee, cocoa, and corn meal containers sumptuously line the shelves among other antique tins and bags in the Wray Museum. Writing Lab photo.

The Wray Museum's General Store, prominently displayed with a coffee grinder near the center, evokes many memories and nostalgic stories from our past. Writing Lab photo.

back to when people would wrap items up in the brown paper and twist one end, making it appear as a cone shape."

When asked about quality and price of today's grocery store items as compared to the early 1900's grocery store items, June remarked that "when people look back at the early 1900's, they think that things were very cheaply priced compared to today's market. But really they weren't. People didn't earn the kind of money that we do today; so in comparison, price is about the same. Also bartering was very common. As for quality, lots of their items were homemade or came fresh off the farm. This is a good aspect because the items didn't have the preservatives and things that some of today's items have, but a lot of their food wasn't able to be kept long because of lack of technology."

June remembers a time when she was growing up. "It was the Fourth of July, sometime in the 1920's, and my father's birthday. One of my father's cousins was a milkman, and he would carry milk from northeastern Colorado to Denver. Well, since it was my father's birthday, it was important that he had ice cream! So my father's cousin brought him the ice cream from Denver packed in dry ice. That way it didn't melt."

She also recalls a time when she went to a "high-society" person's house. "I remember once going to a rich person's house and they had what was known as an ice house. It was an entire building filled with sawdust and enough ice blocks to last for the whole year."

After visiting with June, I got the chance to walk around the general store in the museum and view all the products and items. Many items caught my interest, but a few made me stop and chuckle. When people had stomachaches or indigestion, they couldn't just go and take some Pepto Bismal. Instead they took Black Berry Balsam, a homemade concoction made with blackberry root, white oak bark, Colombo root, rhubarb root, and ginger. For backaches, rheumatism, and kidney disorders, they took Crane's Kidney Pills. For laundering clothes, they used Mrs. Stewart's liquid bluing, whose advertising claimed that clothes turned yellow over time, and Mrs. Stewart's

Products, such as Royal Crystal Salt and Hershey's Cocoa, once used by early residents of this area, now sit on display at the Wray Museum. Writing Lab photo.

A tiny camel stands guard over a display of matches located in the replication of an old General Store in the Wray Museum. Writing Lab photo.

liquid bluing "restored the dingiest clothes to their natural white brightness." In addition, several brands of straw hat dyes in multiple colors, such as jet-black or robin egg blue or scarlet, could be purchased.

While wandering past the clothing section, I remember June had stated, "A lot of people could not afford to go to their general store and buy bolts of cloth. They would instead make their clothes out of the sacks that the flour or sugar would come in. Some families would construct their entire wardrobes from these flour sacks." I found no flour sacks in the clothing section; but instead, numerous bolts of cloth, thread, buttons, and mannequins modeling fashions caught my eye.

Idalia's Old Town Store

Old Idalia's Conrad Mercantile Store, built in 1912, was owned by J.Q. Conrad. This general store wasn't unlike the general stores that June describes. Photos of this general store match the description of having a facade and large display windows. Mr. Conrad ran his store efficiently but encountered money problems with area homesteaders. The *Idalia Centennial* notes that "J.Q. Conrad received much of the land in the Idalia flats area as payment on the bills the homesteaders had accumulated. The homesteaders would come in and throw their deed on J.Q.'s counter and say 'put it against my bill, I'm leaving.' The land at that time was virtually worthless, so it is certain that Mr. Conrad was left with a lot of bills as well as land." (p. 5) This proved to be a trying financial dilemma as Mr. Conrad absorbed a lot of the cost. But if business was good, storekeepers could hold onto their positions as general store owners, and sometimes they even served as postmasters. J.Q. Conrad was the postmaster of his day as well as the general store owner.

Once peered through by the early postmasters of Idalia, this mail window and drop box of the old Idalia Post Office are on display in Elsie Lidke's home. Writing Lab photo.

Putting a post office in a general store served a convenience to the community. It affirmed the adage that "you can kill two birds with one stone" in that people could come into town on one afternoon, buy their supplies, and send and receive their mail without having to travel great distances to accomplish the two tasks. And it wasn't until later in history that the post office separated from the general store and more modern grocery stores caused the old general store to fade into non-existence. Isn't it ironic that today our Super Wal-Marts offer all kinds of merchandise, groceries, toys and dolls, and even postal services?

Dolls, Dolls, Dolls

If we look closely at a photo of Conrad's store, we notice dolls lined up in one window. Ever since the beginning of time, children have spent many hours of leisure time dressing and playing with some sort of doll. Because people often overlook dolls as a part of our history, and part of the history of general stores, let's consider their origin, construction, and importance.

Wearing a frown, a mismatched plastic doll daintily sits and takes in life at the Wray Museum. Writing Lab photo.

Elaborately dressed dolls from several eras quietly reside at their home in the Wray Museum. Writing Lab photo.

Dressed in angelic white lace, a delicate china doll sits in her carriage at the Wray Museum. Writing Lab photo.

A row of beautiful dolls line the right window off the Old Idalia General Store, built in 1921 by J.Q. Conrad. Photo courtesy of Idalia Centennial 1887-1987.

June Redman, once again, told me a story, this one about the origin of dolls. "Dolls have been around since the beginning of time. It is believed that dolls first originated in the days of the pharaohs." June stated that "actual children were at first sacrificed and buried with the pharaohs in hopes that they would have a child with them in their afterlife. Eventually it became unacceptable to kill small children, so the Egyptians used childlike dolls, which they constructed from clay moldings, in place of the sacrificed children. Dolls, even from the earliest stage, have been made from anything, even something as simple as a stick wrapped in cloth. Children just wanted the joy of having a doll; it didn't really matter to them what it was made out of."

Just as June stated, dolls were made out of anything and everything. Wood, cloth, and deerskin provided doll material. Some were even made out of dried apples to resemble the elderly. But most commonly in rural areas, dolls were made from cornhusks. Later, most dolls were constructed from plastic; but due to decay, the plastic would sometimes rot and discolor. June said, "Dolls made from plastic usually were discolored and mismatched anyway because most dolls were produced in parts and then later assembled. Since the parts often came from different factories, the head and body were often two different colors."

It has always been said that dolls are a "girl thing." Especially in the late 1800's and early 1900's, parents encouraged their daughters to have and care for a doll because they believed dolls helped girls practice how to become good mothers. Girls also learned another "home-based" skill by sewing clothes for their dolls.

But dolls are also enjoyed by adults. June couldn't recall any doll stories from her childhood, but she does have her favorite dolls now, especially one called Cissy. "Cissy is a doll straight out of the 50's. She is dressed in a royal blue outfit and is a gorgeous and elaborate doll. She has been my favorite for quite sometime but has to live in a box out of sight due to the little people running around my house."

Dolls were also made elaborately in the late 1800's and early 1900's. Some dolls were so expensive and well dressed that only adults were allowed to play with them because they feared the children would break them. These dolls were specially ordered out of magazines displayed in the general stores.

General store merchandise, post offices, and dolls may seem to have nothing in common; but in truth, they all originated from the same source, the old general stores that have faded into history.

Sources:
June Redman, Wray, Colorado
Idalia Centennial, 1887-1987
Kalman, Bobbie. *Old-Time Toys*. New York: Crabtree
    Publishing Company, 1995.

Ghost Towns in Yuma County

By
Neil Hutton

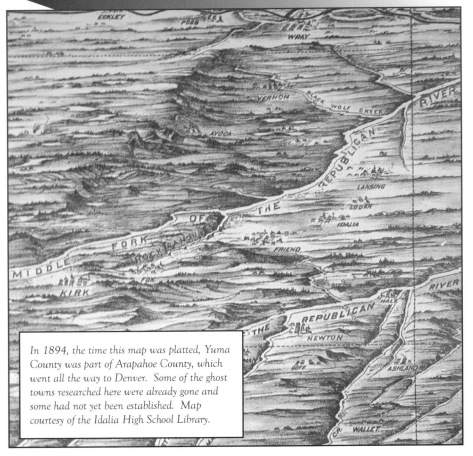

In 1894, the time this map was platted, Yuma County was part of Arapahoe County, which went all the way to Denver. Some of the ghost towns researched here were already gone and some had not yet been established. Map courtesy of the Idalia High School Library.

I chose to write on ghost towns for a couple of reasons. I really wanted to know how many such towns were located around here and where exactly they were located. I had been researching Bonny, Colorado, before this year and decided this would be a good time to continue that research and expand a little. I have always been interested in ghost towns.

Small towns continue to die, yet we know little of the past ghost towns. Hundreds of towns existed between the years of 1890 and 1930; then most disappeared without a bit of evidence. Once thriving communities, many of their deaths resulted from a combination of the golden age of trains and automobiles and the desperate years of drought and depression. Many towns began in the hope that the railroad would go through and bring business. Some towns started as just a little post office and then gained a general store and expanded rapidly; but then automobiles became affordable, and many people could travel to the cities where food and other products were cheaper. Also the drought and depression of the 1930's made people think they could do better in the big cities and soon moved away.

Towns usually owned a post office, but they did not necessarily have to have one to be called a town. Often someone's farm building served as the post office. Sometimes these post offices also sold groceries. But not much information is available on many of these towns because they have been ghost towns for so long that the people who lived in them have died. Also, not much was written about these towns because there were so many that they were not considered unusual enough to write about; that's the very problem I faced while researching this topic.

The towns I researched include Armel, Beecher Island, Friend, Happyville, Heartstrong, Jake-way, Lansing, Leslie, Mildred, Nashville, Schramm, and Bonny. Many other towns that I did not cover are Abarr, Alvin, Avoca, Brownsville, Burdett, Clarksville, Crystal Springs, Ford, Fox, Gurney, Hughes, Logan, Ludlum, Robb, Robber

Roost, Steffins, Wauneta, Wages, Waverly, and Weld City. All of these towns, except Bonny, once existed in Yuma County. Some other towns may have existed in the county at one time or another, but I found no information to that effect.

Armel

Armel, first founded when Armel S. Breninger started his store in 1902, also included the post office for the surrounding area. Although this general store lasted at least until 1960, the post office closed in 1948. Though Armel did not become much of a town, big things did happen there. One of these was the Fourth of July celebration. Over five hundred people usually arrived to play ball, race horses, and even shoot fireworks on this day.

Beecher Island

The Armel Store was more than just a good place to buy supplies. It also served very well as a conversation center. Photo courtesy of the Wray Museum.

Beecher Island started with a post office in 1902. The home of O. E. Ekberg, a dugout, provided the post office. Then in 1925 the first store opened. For ten years a museum, started in 1956 and finally shut down in 1966, was located at Beecher Island. Today the artifacts and information preside at the Wray Museum. The school first operated by donations and fundraisers, not by funding from the state

During a busy day at the Beecher Island mechanical shop, a mechanic works on a Ford Ferguson (Fordson). Photo courtesy of Idalia Community Photo Exhibit.

Beecher Island started with a post office in 1902 and became a ghost town around the 1960's. Photo courtesy of the Wray Museum.

at all. Most of the money came from four local residents, and the school could operate for four months on forty dollars. Then in 1949 the Beecher students rode to Wray for school. The only blacksmith shop was started in 1933 by Orba Brown, and it was still in operation in 1969 by his son.

Friend

Friend was located by the Kansas line in the southeast part of Yuma County. In 1886 a few farmers from Friend, Nebraska, settled there and started a four-homestead center. Friend got its name from the settlers' Quaker religion. One source indicated that Friend had another name: Frontier Legion (*Ghosts of the Colorado Plains*).

A few reporters once called Friend a boomtown because many people chose to settle there. When July of 1887 rolled around, Friend was incorporated and had about twenty buildings. These buildings included a restaurant, two livery stables, a bank, two general stores, two hotels, a saloon, a drug store, and even a newspaper company. Water could be found at the town well. Mail was even delivered from Haglier twice a week.

A school, also used for a church and a meeting hall, was built by the settlers. Although not many people actually lived in the town, it served a very large area of an estimated two hundred people. Friend had been built in anticipation of a railroad coming through their area; but as frequently happened, a train never came and the town was abandoned. Most of the buildings were either torn down or moved to separate farms.

Happyville

Happyville lay twelve miles south of Eckley and twenty-six miles southwest of Wray. Richard Gilmore, who moved to Colorado because of health problems, started the town. He thought that a post office was needed for the area and, to prove his point, he carried the mail without any salary for three months. Finally an official post office was established around 1910. The barn of Richard Gilmore served as the post office, and soon it also provided a creamery, storage for oil, and seed and feed for purchase. Later the town got a machine shop and a garage. Then a barbershop was established, followed by a schoolhouse in 1911. A local farmer saw the need for education and built the schoolhouse. As many as twenty-five people lived in Happyville at one time. The town split because of differing opinions, and that gave birth to the town of Heartstrong.

Heartstrong

Cleve Mason founded Heartstrong. He first ran a store in Happyville, but later he moved his store and three houses to the new Heartstrong. Heartstrong could be found seven miles east and twelve miles south of Yuma. The store moved by Cleve served as a general store, a dance hall, and even a pumping station. Cleve by himself also built another store, garage, creamery, and post office for Heartstrong. Similar in population to Happyville, at least twenty-five people lived in Heartstrong. As in most towns this size, people liked to get together for dances and other activities. They would dance one night, and then the next day they would participate in horse races, ball games, and other entertainment. In 1929 the town started to die out because people moved their houses and business buildings.

A proud owner shows off his general store, gas station, and creamery in Heartstrong, Colorado. Photo courtesy of Wray Museum.

The town did not disappear at this time, but it did not have the partying that it usually did.

Some interesting stories came out of Heartstrong. Only one marriage was conducted there, but the father of the bride was so angry that he carried a shotgun during the services! Even a circus came to Heartstrong, although it never performed there; it started to rain and didn't stop for a week, so the circus moved and performed in Wray. Another story tells that one of the residents bought a Chevrolet coupe with all the rabbit skins he sold.

Jake-way

Jake-way consisted of a saloon, which straddled the Kansas-Colorado state line straight west of Kanorado. Law men from one or the other state could find outlaws in the saloon; but the outlaws could step across the state line while still in the saloon, and the law men could not arrest them.

Lansing

Lansing, Colorado, was founded around 1886. It became a fairly large town with many stores and businesses, which included a hardware store, a general store, a post office, a lumberyard, two small hotels, a photo gallery, two livery barns, and a printing office which published the *Lansing Lariat* newspaper. One of the first postmasters was Asa Beam.

A tornado hit Lansing on Memorial Day 1895, and the town sustained considerable damage. Although many buildings were destroyed, the settlers rebuilt with scraps of lumber thrown around by the storm. After the storm, the same person ran the post office and general store. A few stories about the storm still survive: Frank Reecks was riding his horse home when the tornado picked up him and his horse and carried them over half a mile. A rug was almost pulled out through a window. A wife would not go out to the barn and milk the cow after the tornado, so her husband had to bring the cow up to the house for her to milk it.

Leslie

Leslie was founded two miles south of Logan County and on the Washington-Yuma County line, in the anticipation of the Burlington Railroad line that ran between Holyoke and Akron coming their way. In Leslie's case, the railroad seemed very promising and even resulted in a well being dug for the steam engines' stop. Leslie quickly became a good-sized town. Houses went up, along with a post office, a blacksmith shop, and even a school and a church. A newspaper, called the *Cactus,* was founded; but another source indicates the newspaper was called the *Leslie News* or *Leslie Herald (Ghosts of the Colorado Plains).*

But soon word spread around that a railroad line would not come through after all! This resulted in the general store being moved to Sterling for use as a house because the store could only do a few cents of business in one day, and some days not do any. A few people tried to make a town out of it anyway, but the majority of the people left and soon the town became a ghost. It was founded in 1888 and only lasted until 1892, becoming referred to as a railroad boomtown.

Mildred

Mildred sprang up in 1910, named in honor of a pretty lady of that area. It had a mail route from Vernon even before mail routes were officially established. The local farmers would travel to Vernon to pick up the mail and then take it to the Mildred post office.

Along with the mail, they transported goods to the Mildred store when it was established and run by Archie Kindred. Then by 1911, Mildred had its own post office. The town grew quite well and soon became very populated, but it did qualify as a boomtown because its life span was only eight years.

In those eight years Mildred saw two general stores, a pool hall, a blacksmith shop, and a dance hall. The school for this town was three quarters of a mile away and also served as a church for that area. Some fifty families used this town during its peak size. Even though Mildred served such a small community, it was a lively place with Fourth of July celebrations and a decent baseball team. As still happens today, the town slowly disappeared because people could drive their cars to get cheaper and better groceries and supplies else-where. Eventually the post office and general stores combined into one, and then the post office moved a few more times before it finally discontinued in 1954.

Nashville

Nashville had a store and post office where Delmar Moellenberg's farm is presently located. In fact, the Nashville post office sat where Delmar's chicken house now sits. Clarence Lidke once lived in the old, tin post office; then later he used it as a garage. Delmer and Clarence are both residents of the Idalia area.

Schramm

In 1887 Dr. Raimon Von Herron Schramm came to this area and planned to settle here. He first came and lived in Yuma, but soon left because of hard feelings that developed due to his not becoming the mayor of Yuma. He thought that he should be the mayor because of all the money he had put into the town. Dr. Schramm had a very good reason because he had put more than $50,000 into the businesses there. When he found out that he had not been elected the mayor, he started to move his frame buildings; but before he could tear down his brick buildings, the citizens of Yuma declared that he really was their new mayor. The frame buildings, which he moved from Yuma, became the town of Schramm. That town no longer exists, but it was located where Schramm Feed Lot is today, ten miles east of Yuma on Highway 34.

With this many towns appearing in one county, one realizes why the native American Indians had cause for concern. During the period from 1890 to 1930, eastern Colorado was just as populated as western Colorado. All these small towns had big hopes of growing, but for numerous reasons people either moved or did not patronize their town anymore. Almost all could be called boomtowns because they only lasted a few years and then faded into ghost towns. Some became as big as two hundred in population and then disappeared. In just a few years, any evidence that some of these towns once existed was either torn down, moved, or destroyed by nature.

Bonny, Kit Carson County, Colorado

Bonny, Colorado, of course is not in Yuma County, but its history fascinates me because I live near where the town used to be. In fact, a house is still standing there. The remains of Bonny can be found on the northeast corner of Kit Carson County. Established on June 3, 1915, and disbanded on February 19, 1924, it never really became much more than a post office and a small general store. Velma Bonny lived in Bonny, Colorado, the town that got its name from her ancestors.

In her book, *Bonny, Colorado: A High Plains Ghost Town*, she recalls that Maud Bonny, her mother, was a very small lady, so small that she could walk right under the arm of Jacob, her husband. One evening Maud made dinner for her family, and she then went up to her bedroom saying she was sick. After the family started to eat, Jacob went up to Maud's room and found she had died. She died in 1918, of an unknown cause, at only thirty-seven years of age and left behind six children who ranged from ten months to ten years of age.

After Maud's funeral the four youngest, all five years of age and under, went to Jacob's brother Isaac Bonny and his wife Laura. Jacob and his two oldest children William and Louis went on farming a section of land. Later Jacob tried to get his four other children back, and Velma remembers sitting in the front row of the court house and getting sick because of her fear of leaving Laura. Velma also remembers sister Velda teasing her for crying. Velma recalled, "Papa was such a gentle man. He must have been as scared as we were" (Jacobs, et. al., pg. 10).

Three of Jacob's youngest children were given back to him, and the little girls got beaded purses. The children he got back after the court case were Velma, Velda, and Mildred. Velda and Velma remember stopping at Saltair, a resort near Salt Lake City, where the three got carved walnut shells. Velma put hers in her purse, and she treasured that purse until losing it in a flooded room when she lived in Clearmont, Wyoming.

The twins, Mildred and Velda, clearly remember sitting in the back of the Model T and being filled with uncertainty about what was going to happen to them. Vernon, Mildred's brother, was still an infant when his mother died; so he lived with Isaac and Laura in Idaho, and later they adopted Vernon. He had no memory of his parents.

Being in a store with large mirrors for the first time remained one of Velda's clearest memories. Velda clearly saw Mildred, but that was not where Mildred was. Mirrors were such a new experience that, for a while, it looked like Mildred had a twin. Ironically, the town of Bonny now has not a twin but a descendent which carries its name. Bonny Dam, which lies about six miles south of Idalia, got its name from this small town.

Sources:
Eberhart, Perry. *Ghosts of the Colorado Plains*.
    Athens, Ohio: Swallow Press, 1986.
Jacobs, Velma Bonny, et.al. *Bonny, Colorado: A High Plains Ghost Town* .
    Greeley, Colorado: Smallest Room Press, 1995.
Shorty Wilcoxen's notes with Idalia Writing Lab Archives.
Yuma County Historical Society. *Action On The Plains*.
    Yuma, Colorado: Pioneer Printing, 1971.

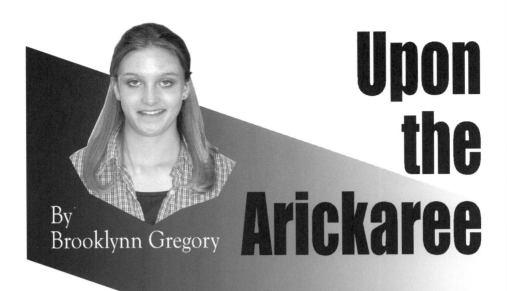

Upon the Arickaree

By
Brooklynn Gregory

A crumbling homestead rests on the Mullin Ranch,
about ten miles west of the original frame house.
Writing Lab photo.

When I came into our Writing Lab class, I didn't really know what to expect. Writing short stories to read in front of the school? A type of speech class? Writing poems? However, I soon helped decide that we would research something about this area of Colorado. Because I just moved here about a year ago from Loveland, and I had never lived on a ranch before, I decided to research the history of the Mullin Ranch on which I live. I want to thank Billie Poenisch for all of the information she gave me on that ranch. And I am grateful for the information I found in the Idalia Centennial. *Doing this research has given me a "sense of roots" very quickly because I now know more about this place where I live.*

Along the Arickaree River lies a ranch settled in 1886, the Mullin Ranch. The Fox Ranch was settled a year earlier, so that makes the Mullin Ranch the second oldest in this area. What is now 7,000 acres of land, three miles west and five miles north of Idalia, first started as 160 acres of a homestead.

I'm sure most people know what a homestead is; but for those who do not, it is "a house, especially a farmhouse, with adjoining buildings and land." The land is "claimed by a settler or a squatter, especially under the Homestead Act." The Homestead Act was

The remains of a homesteader's barn lie on the east side of the old homestead on the Mullin Ranch. Writing Lab photo.

passed by Congress in 1862 promising the ownership of a 160-acre tract of public land to a head of a family after he cleared and improved the land and lived on it for five years." (*American Heritage Dictionary*) A Homestead Law is "any of several laws in most states exempting a householder's homestead from attachment or forced sale to meet general debts" (*American Heritage Dictionary*). "Anyone was able to claim up to 320 acres of land" (*Idalia Centennial*, p. 5).

In the *Idalia Centennial*, former Idalia resident Charles D. Shields says, "In the 1870's and early 1880's, this country had the appearance of being the most ideal grazing range that any cattleman could wish for. In the sand hills at that time, the sage brush was no menace. In the rough sand hills there grew a grass we called 'sand hill grass,' and on the more level ground a high grass called 'red bunch grass' grew. The hard land and rough breaks were covered with grama and buffalo grass. Along the streams were great meadows of blue joint grass with other meadows of shorter, finer textured grasses. On the hard land flats a heavy coat of buffalo grass grew four to five inches tall-just a perfect mat." (p. 24) That type of grazing range no doubt attracted homesteader to what is now known as the Mullin Ranch.

This ranch used to be the Shields/Davisson Ranch and later became known as the Jack Mullin Ranch. However, when the ranch was first settled, it was known as the Wineglass Ranch. Bill Diss, an attorney in Denver and a native of Wray, now owns the Wineglass brand. Some people say this ranch was a stage stop at one time.

Now Ina Mullin and the Poenisch family own the ranch. Billie says, "This started out as a homestead, and there were several ranches both down east and west; but I don't know how it was compiled because I have never gotten to see the abstracts to know when it was bought and how." The Mullin Ranch was also a mail stop at one time, known as Shields, Colorado. Billie says, "Tommie Wilcoxen said that he carried the mail up the Arickaree River, by horseback, to the Fox's...The Fox Ranch was Fox, Colorado." Tommie was one of Idalia's mail route carriers.

Billie and Clayton have a brand which features an upside-down

Homesteaders Mr. and Mrs. Daniel Shields established the Shields Ranch, now known as the Mullin Ranch. Wray Museum photo.

Behind the old homestead sits this rock-surrounded well which homesteaders no doubt used for their water supply. Writing Lab photo.

and backward P with a C underneath it. Clayton wanted a brand with only two letters so he used his initials. Another brand on the ranch, the Lazy J, belonged to Jack Mullin (Billie's father); and now Carl Poenisch, Clayton's son, owns it.

My mother Mickie, my sister Erin, my stepfather Brent, and I live in the original frame house on the ranch. Built in 1907, this house now has a Ranch Style addition that was constructed in 1967 by Billie and Clayton. However, before they could add on to the house, they had to knock down a three-room, rock and sod building that had been erected in 1886. When Billie and Clayton knocked down the old building, they found two layers of sod pressed together in one

This spring house, built in 1886, served as a "refrigerator" on the Mullin Ranch.
Writing Lab photo.

corner with the grass between the layers still green. That means that the sod was sitting in that building for eighty-one years, from 1886 to 1967!

Another original building on the ranch is a spring house that sits east of the house in which I live. It too was built in 1886. The *American Heritage Dictionary* says a spring house is "a small house constructed over a spring and used to keep food cool." Billie said, "The spring house was used as a refrigerator, keeping milk and butter cool as it sat in the water. It is still a nice place for watermelons."

The water that flows from the hill behind my house used to run into the spring house. Billie said, "We worked to try and get all the water out because it was rotting the foundation and we wanted the spring house to still stand, but I think the water is still there. It still comes up and the spring runs out onto the yard right by your house. If you keep it clean, then it does real well. The spring then goes underground and comes up by the barn. There is also a spring, in between our house and yours, which is under the trees."

In the pasture are many rock bluffs and a picnic area that Billie calls Spring Creek, and one has to cross a spring-fed creek to get there. "Rose Ramseier, Mark Ramseier's great aunt, used to be the postmistress here," said Billie. "She said that when she was young they had all the picnics up there. Later, in the late 50's and early 60's, the high school students took hay rides down here on this ranch and then picnicked up at Spring Creek. We built a permanent table up there and a fire circle."

Also, Billie said that "the 4-Hers used to have picnics down at Box Canyon. They had a trail to ride that would start up by the Fox Ranch, which was the Bowman's then, and all the kids would ride the horses down the river and end up at Box Canyon to camp out." The reason it is called Box Canyon is because the hills around it were used to box in cattle. "I think there was a homestead down there because there is a grave with a fence around it. Leo McCoy's mother told me that the grave belonged to a baby of some homesteaders that were down there at one time," Billie said.

As people come onto the Mullin Ranch, they can see a Buffalo Hunter's grave up on the hill. A few years ago, the Colorado Historical Society placed a marker near the outline of the grave, but one could see where the buffalo hunter's grave lay even before that marker was put down. Billie believes the Kiowa and Cheyenne might have lived in this area but she isn't sure. "Leo McCoy said that years ago you could see where the ceremonial fires had been and where the buffalo were across the creek," said Billie. The McCoys were neighbors to the Poenischs.

A barn also sits near the house. Billie heard the barn had burned at one time and then was rebuilt. "During the Flood of 1935, the barn was able to withstand it. The water got up inside of the barn, but it was not washed away," she said.

Billie also said they once had two little springs on the property, but she didn't know any details about their importance. The *Idalia Centennial*, on the other hand, has an entire page of information on

Beneath the rocks and dirt, inside the boundaries of the Mullin Ranch, lies an unknown Buffalo Hunter who died in the 1870's. Writing Lab photo.

the two little springs, on both their legend and phenomenon. The two springs were situated on the north side of the Arickaree River, where Daniel Shields had established the Shields Ranch (now the Mullin Ranch). The phenomenon of the springs is "the source, the temperature and purity of the water... The hill, from which these springs exit, seems to be of soft magnesia rock. Just below the level of the springs there is a thin, almost water-tight 'hard pan' which forces the water to the outlets of the two springs." In earlier years when people were digging the first wells, the water of the wells seemed to be warmer than that of the spring water. Also a strip of hillside about fifteen to thirty feet wide "extending up the hill from the hard pan...was always wetter than the ground." (*Idalia Centennial*, p. 58)

So where did this water originate? These springs were on relatively level plain, but their source is about 200 to 250 miles away from the nearest mountains or high timberline peaks. "I can only make a guess as to the source and that guess is extremely far fetched. We know that there is a shale formation extending from the mountains eastward at least as far as the Kansas-Nebraska line," says Charles D. Shields in the *Idalia Centennial*. A few years later when Charles returned to where the springs had been, he observed, "Due to the lack of use they had deteriorated to a condition that seemed to make them completely useless." (*Idalia Centennial*, p. 58)

From prairie grasses to a homestead to an old ranch house surrounded with original buildings and springs, the Mullin Ranch spans many years and several name changes. And many people have walked over the acres: Native American Indians, buffalo hunters, school children, and various families. I sincerely hope the ranch will continue to offer a unique history and way of life.

Sources:
Billie Poenisch, Idaila, Colorado
Chuck Brandon's letter to the Writing Lab, April 4, 1999.
"Idalia 100 Years Old." *Idalia Centennial 1887-1987.*
"Ranching." *Idalia Centennial 1887–1987*
Shields, Charles D. "The Legend and Phenomenon of the Two Little Springs" (from Tommie Wilcoxen's Notes). *Idalia Centennial 1887–1987*

Early Day Telephones

By
Brooklynn Gregory

In the 1950's telephone callers cranked out a series of long and short rings, individually coded to each party on a line. The "crank" (not visible here) hung on the right side of the phone. Photo courtesy of Dennis Schiel.

Many years ago, people did not have the luxury of being able to push little numbered buttons and have the person they wanted magically appear on the end of a line. Many people didn't even have a phone; but if they did, it would have been a crank telephone or whatever was available at that time. The Kirk telephone system started around 1907 with only four lines. "The first pass switch at Idalia was at the Chas. Ingalls home southwest of town." There were only three of these particular lines. But finally on July 23, 1953, the Plains Cooperative Telephone Association was formed. (*Idalia Centennial*, p. 33)

When Billie and Clayton Poenisch first moved to our area, they had an old crank telephone. Their number was 6 F3. That means they were on Line Six, and they had three long rings; but it didn't always work. "The telephone office used to be in Idalia where the Collins' place was, next to the post office. But sometimes we would try to make a call and the operator wouldn't be there. She wasn't there all that often," said Billie. "The operator's grandmother would be there, so she would ask which party number you were because there were six party numbers on that line. After a while she would ask if you wanted the operator, and then she would go find her. The operator would finally get on the phone and place your call. If you wanted to make a long distance call, it would take even longer because the operator would have to repeat everything said. The reason she would have to repeat is because the phone lines were so bad."

They got the new phones in 1961, and that is when Billie started substituting for the Idalia School. (She substituted for twenty years at the Idalia High School.) Before the new telephones were installed, the school didn't really have any reliable way of contacting substitutes, and it took too much time to use the crank telephones because the operator wasn't always there.

Bill Carpenter of rural Idalia also gave some information on telephones in a letter he wrote to the Writing Lab on October 20, 2001.

Bill, his mother, and his brother moved to Idalia in 1954. They lived here until 1961 but then moved away. Then Bill and his mother returned in 1980. Mable Carpenter, Bill's mother, who passed away in 1990, was the Idalia operator from 1954 to 1957 or 1958. "I remember each telephone number was coded as a long ring and a short ring, one long and two shorts, or three shorts and three long rings, etc.," Bill writes. Bill also remembers when there were about ten lines, with seven to ten parties on each line.

If there was a storm outside, one couldn't hear anything with all

The first telephone switch board in the Idalia Exchange of the early 1900's can still be viewed at Elsie Lidke's home in Idalia. Writing Lab photo.

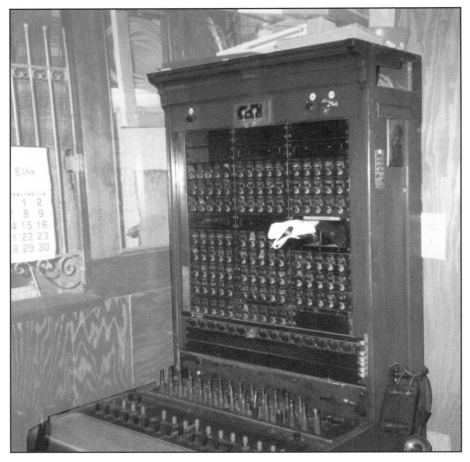

the noise that was in the line. Since people could listen in on other people's conversations, one would have to talk over all of that commotion too. Bill continues his letter by saying his mother would have to ask everyone to hang up, except the ones who were talking in the first place, and that would help with the noise. The operator also used a "general ring" which consisted of a series of ten rings. If an announcement had to be made, Mable would use the "general ring" and then everyone could pick up their phones and hear the announcement. The announcement could be telling about an upcoming basketball game or alerting students that school was canceled due to a storm.

I think our society has benefited greatly from the technology used for telephones. It is faster and easier, and we don't have to tolerate noise on the line. Today we can have a private conversation with those to whom we want to talk. Many years ago, talking on the telephone was like telling an entire community one's news. Now we can even talk to people over the Internet by using a phone hook-up for our modem. However, we are not talking; we are typing. I don't think I could handle not being able to reach someone quickly, especially if it were an emergency. So I am proud of our growth in technology because we are able to use phones in a way that could not have been possible just a few short years ago.

Sources:
Billie Poenisch, Idalia, Colorado
Bill Carpenter's letter to the Writing Lab, October 20, 2001
"Excerpts from the History of the Telephone in Yuma County"
   (from Tommie Wilcoxen's Notes). *Idalia Centennial 1887 –1987.*

Unseen, But Not Forgotten

By
Jobediah Rittenhouse

The sod house built
in 1910 by Walter Zion
became the basis for my story.
The house has survived over ninety years
and still remains in good condition.
Writing Lab photo.

When this year's Writing Lab class started and we decided to write a book, I was not very excited about what was to come. I wasn't worried about the writing part of the article. I was more concerned over my lack of interest in the heritage of Idalia as a community. I read through the first two Gusts of Dust books and looked through parts of the Idalia Centennial: 1887-1987 newspaper. Still, none of the history seemed to grasp my attention as "exciting and interesting." I realize the lack of respect I showed to the people who went through the hardship of coming to this area, starting with nothing, and making it go. Then, as a member of a school organization, I went to a sod house that was donated to our local, non-profit foundation to clean and help keep it maintained. While cleaning this house, I started to realize that, strangely, someone had lived there and, even more incredibly, that it was built almost one hundred years ago by using just blocks of dirt. This "inspired" me to write about sod houses and, in particular, Joe Zion's sod house.

In the spring of 1909, Walter Zion and his wife Anna left the city of Denver to move from the urban life to a calm and more peaceful rural lifestyle. Walter was never a city person, and he wanted to live nearer to his parents in eastern Colorado. He left Denver with only forty-five dollars in cash and just enough furniture for a five-room house. Bringing his wife and three children, he traveled through Wray and ended up in a small, native rock house of only two rooms on the Copper-Kettle River northwest of Idalia.

That home, on the Wilmath Place, was where Joe Zion, their fourth child, was born in 1909. This portion of land was "given" to them by the government as part of the Homestead Act of 1865. The term "given" is used loosely because the land was, in fact, not handed over to them at all. To quote Joe from an interview, "...Give it to ya? Hell! You don't know what those people went through to go out there on that land and, you know, start with nothin' just out on the prairie and build a home."

Then with a home found but money being somewhat of a problem, Walter worked at any job he could get. Although times were hard, the Zion family toughed it out; and then in the fall of 1910, they moved into a sod house built by Walter. They lived in that home for thirty-four years until December 8, 1944, when he and Anna moved to Wray and left the homestead to their son Joe. They had lived out on their original homestead longer than any other families around. They lived through years of drought; tolerated pestilence of rabbits, grasshoppers, and prairie chickens; and refused to give up. "I admire my parents for that. I couldn't have done it," said Joe.

Joe's Home, Sweet Home

Joseph A. Zion was born in the small, two-room rock house on July 3, 1909, and later he moved with his family into the sod house built by his father. Joe now lives in a small house in Wray, Colo-

Joe Zion, 93, sits in his favorite chair in his home in Wray, Colorado. Up until November of 1975, he lived in and owned a sod house that is located about fifteen miles northwest of Idalia near the Mullin Ranch. Writing Lab photo.

rado, about thirty miles north of Idalia. On November 27, 2001, I interviewed him at his home and used that interview for the basis of this story.

Joe is a small, frail man in his 90's; and although he is nearing the later stages of his life, the memories of his younger years are as strong as ever. He described the time when he lived in the sod house as the "best years" of his life, and the house was more like "an old friend" than just a roof over his head. He was and still remains regretful that he was forced to sell that house. "It broke my heart, but that's life," he said. But as he aged, it became less and less habitable for him, understandably so. In November of 1975, he sold the property to Clayton Poenisch at an auction, and it was "the hardest thing I had ever done in my ninety-plus years!" Joe lived in the soddy from the time he was about two years old until September 15, 1975.

The home he lives in now compares in many ways to the house of sod that he lived in years ago. This house too contains merely the essentials. And it is small and quaint, much like the soddy he inhabited in his youth. As one enters his house, he sees to the right of the door a small plaque that was given to Joe at last year's family reunion, honoring him at the age of ninety-two as the oldest member of the Zion family. The main rooms consist of simply a kitchen and his bedroom, and these two rooms have shrunk in size because they are now more insulated than the others. The other rooms of the house are rarely visited and, because they don't retain heat well, are generally used for storage.

Joe sat in a small, green chair almost directly across from a century-old piano that sits in his bedroom. He is very talkative and, while he showed me a scrapbook that he kept, I grew amazed at the details he recalls from photos that were taken over half a century ago. Although Joe rarely visits the home of his youth, the memories live on with him. But he did visit the old home this past year during his family reunion (referred to above) held in that area. Because of the secluded area in which the sod house sits and due to his fragile health, Joe has not been able to visit the house as often as I am sure he would prefer.

Despite the age of the sod house, the building has stayed in very good condition due to the excellent care Joe had previously given it. In 1948, he covered the building with four to ten inches of cement to keep the heat in during the cold, winter months. Joe also described the structure of his current home, and oddly enough the walls here have also been thickly insulated by him, along with the ceiling and roof. I found this somewhat amusing because, although Joe applied the insulation to keep heat in and cold out, I wonder if he wasn't "driven" to insulate these walls also. However, although Joe didn't realize it when he cemented the sod walls, he was preserving a piece of history for generations to come.

The Journey West

In the 1800's, as more and more people began to move out onto the High Plains to settle and raise their families, they soon came to realize that life on the plains differed very much from the lifestyle that belonged to their past generations in the East. The few trees on the plains made it impossible to erect log cabins, and other housing techniques weren't usable because of a lack of resources. Another problem that settlers soon discovered on the plains was the lack of rainfall and rivers; because of this, homesteads couldn't always be positioned near water, so necessary for crops and human consumption.

Even today, as one heads east on Highway 36 from Denver, the landscape is quite similar to that which was seen by the early settlers of this region. Homesteaders met miles and miles of a vast prairie with rarely a tree in sight. Therefore, the very first people to brave the West and stake their claim built their homes from the little timber that was present. Then, because of the intense climate, land near water was next to be claimed; and what was left was nothing but an unending sea of prairie. But homesteaders soon found methods to overcome these tremendous odds. One such way was to build houses out of sod. They erected these types of homes by using materials that were, in fact, as "dirt" cheap as could be found. Using soil and grasses, along with other materials, settlers created homes where once nothing stood; and soon these types of homes started to spread across eastern Colorado and all over the High Plains.

Today, as people travel on the roads and highways in eastern Colorado, they frequently see the remains of sod houses and other such buildings sitting in pastures and fields. As I began my research for this story, I found an overwhelming number of pictures of sod houses in this region. The sod walls were made very thick in order to create a habitable environment and add to the overall strength of the home. The sod, along with the grasses, provided a strong, yet flexible, form of building material. Not only were the walls of the homes made of sod but, many times, the roofs also. This type of housing was used quite often in the prairie states in the early to late 1800's.

However, as lumber became more readily available as the population began to grow, these homes became used less and less often. Soon, nearly all the sod houses became abandoned, and now they sit in pastures along roads. In fact, very few remain in very good condition; and with the crumbling of the houses, comes the fading of the history and heritage of our ancestors who settled the area in which we now live.

A Home Left to the Land

One of the many sod houses built in this area is the one constructed by Walter Zion in 1910. This house is similar in design to other soddies built all over the plains at that time. The type of soil Walter used for his home was "alkali soil" which he got from "Hay Gulch," about three miles away from the sod house site. According to Joe and some Internet websites, alkaline soil was the best type of soil to use because it contained many roots, which held the soil together very well. The sod was cut into blocks and stacked to form a

Pictures taken by Joe show the Zion property in 1950 (top) and 1952. The three buildings of sod in the background still remain today. The windmill doesn't stand any longer, but lies near the buildings. Photos courtesy of Joe Zion.

house structure.

When the Zion family moved into this new home in 1910, their floor was dirt and they used curtains to separate the small home into three rooms. But their piano also made the Zion residence a popular place to gather. With radio nonexistent and television unknown, a piano provided a wonderful source of entertainment. Joe described their home as the place where people gathered around the holidays and when people just wanted to relax. This special piece of furniture, this piano, which they bought in Denver for $137, is the one that still remains in Joe's present home and is now over one hundred years old. Joe, a former piano tuner, keeps the antique piano in excellent condition; and from what I have heard, he remains very talented at playing the piano even as he ages. Years ago, this piano helped the family enjoy themselves when all their work was done at the end of the day. And people often visited the Zion home, not only because of the piano but also because the sod house was a nice, cozy place to stay. Teachers who needed boarding often stayed at the

Zion house, as did any preachers passing through.

As years passed, the Zion family made renovations to their home by using cement and later one-by-twelve inch boards to make a floor. Joe easily remembers this time because he always lost pencils and other narrow objects through the cracks in the floorboards. Many years later this floor was torn out in order to put in custom floorboards, and Joe remembers having to clean out all of the dirt that had seeped underneath the original wooden boards.

That house was not the only sod building on the Zion residence. Although he could not remember a date, Joe recalls that their bunkhouse, or what they called "the den," was built for his older brother Leonard to use as a room. Later, Leonard moved out; and then Joe and his other brother George used the room for their bedroom. A third building was the milk house also built by Walter. All of the buildings still remain on the land and in excellent condition, especially the main house.

Over the past half-century, the sod house has remained in such excellent condition because of the cement that Joe added on in 1948. The thick cement protected the soil construction from erod-

A small building, one of the three made out of sod by Walter Zion in 1910, was used as a milk house. Writing Lab photo.

This bunkhouse served as the room of Joe's older brother. Like the other two buildings that remain on the property, it is made completely out of sod. Writing Lab photo.

In the late summer of 2001, the Idalia El Pomar Youth in Community Service group cleaned the sod house as a community service project. Writing Lab photo.

ing and falling apart. Joe lived in that house until the early 1970's; and it remained in excellent, livable conditions until 1975 when he sold it to Clayton Poenisch.

From that time until the present, the home has been left dormant and lies quietly like the land that remains unchanged around it. As years passed, the home became a refuge for rats, mice, and other small rodents that no longer had to worry about the threat of humans and so laid claim to the buildings. Because of the isolated area in which this house sits, the land and other precious buildings eventually became forgotten or unknown to most people. All except for Joe, who never forgets the place where he lived for the majority of his life.

Eventually, Clayton Poenisch donated the land to the Idalia Vision Foundation; and in the autumn of 2001, as a community service project, the Idalia Chapter of El Pomar Youth in Community Service went to the sod house to clean it. Although it still needs further cleaning, the small house built of dirt and grass is now more than just a rugged shelter used by rodents. When Joe was told of how the house was being maintained, he was pleased beyond compare, saying, "It's such an honor to my folks."

The soddy is so isolated that one must drive fifteen miles off the highway through twisting dirt roads to reach it. Then only by taking a vehicle on a torn-up pasture road can one get to this secluded spot, where sixty years ago Joe and his family sat around their piano and entertained guests of all kinds. After visiting this former home during his 2001 family reunion, he remarked, "It looks so different, 'cept the lagoon...It broke my heart (seeing the house in such poor shape), but that's life..." Even his descriptions of a small pond where rainwater collects prove to be remarkably clear. As time goes on, these buildings will remain dormant along with countless others like it that lie across eastern Colorado...unforgotten by those who knew them, but unknown to those who didn't.

Even today, as we have entered into a new millennium, things have drastically changed in our area of Colorado. Once an endless sea of prairie rolling in the winds changed to land dotted with scattered homesteads. Now it is covered with small cities and many tiny towns. Around Idalia and other rural areas, although the landscape has somewhat remained the same, the natural heritage to the land has died with the people who first settled it. The vast herds of bison have been replaced with cars because people no longer concern themselves with how they are going to feed their families and make it through the coming winter, focusing instead on what they plan to do for the weekend. Times have changed. For the better or for the worse? I don't know. But I wonder if in eighty years, when my lifetime is coming to an end, whether or not things will have changed enough in technology and other aspects the way they changed during Joe Zion's lifetime. And if they do, will the past be of enough interest to people for them to write a book including what I remember. I guess we'll see.

Sources:
Joseph Zion, Wray, Colorado
Irby, Rebecca LeeAnne and Greetham, Phil. *Laura Ingalls Wilder, Frontier Girl.*
    1998. http://webpages.marshall.edu/~irby1/laura/sodhouse.html
Sod Houses 1998-2002. http://www.websteader.com
Zion, Joseph. "Zion Soddy and Piano." Brief Homestead History.

Idalia's Fashions in the 20's

By
Kendra VanMeter

*Without malls around the corner,
women in the 1920's designed and sewed
much of the clothes their families needed.
Writing Lab photo taken at Wray Museum.*

Gusts of Dust, Volumes I and II, give us lots of information about Idalia's history. But much more history we don't know and may never know. Our books have been about Idalia's past and some of its present, but one part has only been skimmed in Volume I. It's not the most significant part of history, but it is history. What about the fashions? Fashions reflect history, so I wanted to know a little about Idalia's fashions, especially from the 1920's. I know fashions vary greatly for the rich and elite; but I'm sure in the rural areas, many similarities exist between what people wore then and what we wear now because we are mainly a farming community. I also wished to explore what children wore in and out of school.

To get some of the actual fashion information, I searched the Internet; but that only gave what was popular in New York and Paris. I know that is where the trends started, but today people also look to Los Angeles to determine what is popular. Although one can always have "one's own style," it was probably a little difficult out here to know what was "in" at any one time. Now we have the Internet and television to get immediate ideas.

Women's Fashion

In the past, many women made their clothes because they could not just go to a mall to buy a dress for a party, especially around Idalia. They had to buy the patterns (if they even used patterns) and make the clothes themselves or hire a seamstress. As time went on, catalogs offered dresses for sale; for example, in the 1920's dresses sold for eighty-nine cents or a dollar in a Sears, Roebuck Catalog. But even with catalogs, women around Idalia usually made all of the clothes from "material" or "dry goods" priced at eleven cents to thirty-nine cents a yard. Some had sewing machines, operated by a foot pedal; but sewing took time, just like now. And sewing machines were expensive. A "Franklin Electric Rotary" machine in a console cost $60.00, according to a 1926 Sears, Roebuck Catalog. Of course, most women didn't own very many dresses, especially in rural areas. Some had two or three "work dresses" for the week, if that many, and then one special dress for Sunday.

In the 20's, women wanted to become a little more independent. That whole time period in the big cities was associated with having fun, and they wore clothes that expressed that. For the first time in the history of fashion, women began showing a little leg; dresses tended to be baggy and go just past the knee, especially in the early 20's. Cotton and wool were frequently used fabrics. For a more glamorous look, women wore silk and rayon in the cities. But things were a little different here. "When my mother was a child, she had one dress to wear and one to wash," said Gail Mansfield, Idalia teacher. Back then women only wore dresses; they didn't wear slacks. Around the house, a woman always wore a "house dress" and

Sparkling sequins and lace make this jacket a glamorous addition to the Wray Museum. Writing Lab photo.

Ruth Small, teacher at Star School in 1923-1924, wears a stylish, slightly baggy, and lace trimmed dress with some heeled boots. Photo courtesy of Idalia Community Photo Exhibit.

work shoes, even on the farm.

In various places in the 20's, women went for a more boyish look, wearing looser dresses and short hair, such as the bob. Later in the 20's, dresses went higher. Hemlines rose, and bare arms showed.

"In the 30's, hemlines went back down quite far," said June Redman, a volunteer source of information for the Wray Museum. Some people went back to the corsets and other restrictive undergarments because a more conservative look came back. "When women dressed up for church, they usually wore darker colored dresses," said June. The basic dress was black or dark blue with black lace around the bottom. Lace was a very popular fabric then for dressier clothes; even now it is used for fancier items. A jacket at the Wray Museum has lace sewn around the wrists and on various other parts of the jacket, and beads added along the lace give it a glamorous look. Sequins also give this garment a shinier, richer look.

Accessories for Women's Fashion

Fashion includes more than dresses. Women have always paid attention to their attire from the top of their heads to the bottom of their feet, and that also included the mundane task of caring for everything.

As the years went on, hemlines did grow longer, but a certain trend stayed for a while. Women wore dresses, hats, gloves, stockings, and heels for a dress-up occasion. "Hats and gloves were a must," said June. Corsets eventually gave way to girdles and petticoats. In the early 20's some women, mainly city women, wore mink coats, suits, and knee socks.

Most women did their own hair. It would appear that over the years, certain hairstyles became more popular than others. Women usually didn't get to go to a hairdresser any time they wanted to go. June said, "Women did most of it themselves." Most women and girls had curly hair. Some only had curls around the ends; others had curls all over their head. In some cases, a ratty hairstyle was popular, and it will probably always be that way. Some children just don't like doing their hair, or even having it done.

Around the house, women usually wore long aprons over their dresses to try and keep them clean. They had three or four aprons. Then if they had company or if the apron got dirty, they could just put on a clean one. Some aprons tied in the back with a full front. Others had full front and back, with ties on the sides. As the years went on, aprons got smaller. Now we have aprons basically just for cooking or waiting tables in restaurants, and they usually just tie in the back and have pockets to hold things.

Jewelry, like now, was worn for dressy occasions. Sophisticated women in the 20's liked very glamorous jewelry with pearls and gold. Not much silver but more gold was popular. Women would also carry little beaded purses and wear clouch hats in the 20's. Later, hats had bright colors, such as orange, yellow, green, or pink, especially in the 30's. Some of the other colors included black, white, dark blue, and a kind of dark turquoise; but lots of hats were black.

In the 20's women wore stockings of cotton or silk and rayon. They had big seams down the back that women tried to hide or keep straight. Then around the 60's, seamless nylons appeared and panty hose became popular.

Shoes underwent drastic changes during the past century. Earlier shoes looked more like slim boots, usually black and tied up the front. In the 20's, women's dress shoes were usually black or brown pumps of various styles. The popular brown or black Oxford shoe, usually with heels of an inch or an inch and one-half, were work shoes. Around the 40's, women wore anklets with those shoes. Women also wore shoes that were small because it was seen as attractive, but they usually had a good pair that fit properly. Then the heels got slimmer and slimmer. Roberta Moellenberg of rural Idalia said that in the 50's "there was a lot of hard-surface flooring like linoleum, and the companies would just have a fit because a 120-pound woman with a pair of spiked shoes exerted as much force as an elephant on the end of those heels. Linoleum floors always had dents in them from women's spiked heels."

A few women, especially in cities, were fortunate to have vanities. Some things one could find on a vanity included a mirror, combs, and jewelry in jewelry boxes. And especially during hot summers, a fan would also be sitting on a vanity. Another thing found in a woman's room might be an umbrella made out of cloth. These umbrellas weren't just for rain, but they could also be used on a hot day to hinder the sun's rays. Also on shelves in a woman's room might be found hats, gloves, brassieres, shoes, and other feminine necessities.

Hats, resting on hat stands when not worn, and umbrellas were city women's accessories in the 1920's. Writing Lab photo taken at Wray Museum.

Washboards, tubs, and hand-driven ringers helped ease the difficult task of doing the laundry. Writing Lab photo taken at Wray Museum.

After the hassle with the washboards was over, one could buy an electric washing machine, if the area was lucky enough to have electricity. This made laundry chores much easier. Advertisement courtesy of 1926 Sears, Roebuck and Co. Catalog.

Another significant "accessory" to fashion, but rarely associated with "fashion" and never worn, is "the washer." Washing machines, called "electric washers" in 1926, cost $75 from Sears, Roebuck. This was very expensive, but most Idalians didn't have electricity anyway, which meant laundry was done by hand and clothes weren't always very clean. The women had to carry water to the house and heat it, then set a washboard against the side of a tub or bucket, and use that to scrub the clothes. Many different types of washboards had different types of textures. June Redman said, "Because whites got the dirtiest, women put those clothes into a pot on a stove and basically boiled the clothes clean." They also would have to make their own soap out of lye and lard. "Soap wasn't the easiest thing to make, which was another factor of why clothes weren't washed as often back then," said June. They dried the clothes by hanging them on an outdoor clothesline or on a tool hung on the wall that had pieces of wood radiating out from it. (I think now we are pretty spoiled, first getting to just go out and buy soap from a store, and then being able to just stick clothes in a washing machine and a dryer.) In 1926, people lucky enough to have electricity could buy an electric iron for $1.73, but most women had to heat flat irons on their gasoline or kerosene stoves or on the old coal and wood ranges.

Children's Fashion

Some of the children's clothes out here on the Eastern Plains were quite different than those worn in the bigger cities; pictures show the differences. But some similarities also existed. Hairstyles here resembled those of the children in a 1926 catalog. A popular hairstyle for both boys and girls was to part their hair off to the side. The boys would have it slicked back. The girls would usually have it short or going to their chin and often curly. Sometimes both boys and girls would have it slicked down. Some little girls wore knee-length dresses with sweaters over their shoulders. During the winter they wore long cotton stockings and coats that went to their shins.

Proudly standing outside the first Idalia High School building are the school's first graduates in 1927: Clark Elliot, Lena Langendoerfer, Ina V. Moore, Hulda Helling, and Vada Moore. Overalls and baggy dresses were typical attire at that time. Photo courtesy of Idalia Community Photo Exhibit.

The entire 1923-1924 student body poses near the Star School. The children are wearing the overalls and long cotton stockings that many children wore in the 1920's. Photo courtesy of Idalia Community Photo Exhibit.

An advertisement in the March 27, 1908, issue of the Wray Rattler, for the F. Mayer Boot and Shoe Company of Milwaukee, Wisconsin, says that "Special Merit" children's shoes "wear like iron." They were trying to emphasize the good quality of those shoes and how they would last a long time. Today's shoes don't last nearly as long. Copy of ad courtesy of Wray Museum.

Young boys wearing denim overalls and "all over suits," common in the 1920's, are modeling for the 1926 Sears, Roebuck and Co. Catalog. Advertisement courtesy of 1926 Sears, Roebuck and Co. Cata-

Little boys would wear overalls, much like some of the farmers. "All children were expected to change clothes the moment they came home from school," said June. For dressier affairs, some of the boys wore nice pants and white shirts.

Men's Fashion

Farmers wore shirts and denim pants. Sometimes they would wear overalls, not much different from those worn today. When they dressed up in a western suit, they always wore boots and a cowboy hat. Other men, who always had to dress up, wore suits. "Shirts in the 1800's would have detachable collars and cuffs. Some of the collars were high and stiff," said Roberta. "You could take those off and wash them because that was a lot easier. That was what usually got dirty." All men had at least one suit for Sunday, no matter which era. Suits in the twenties were slightly baggy with cuffed pant legs and occasionally a matching vest. "For young men, the casual wear was pants called knickerbockers," said June. These pants were also slightly baggy and came to just below the knees, where the pant legs were gathered. "They would also wear a nice white shirt with a sweater vest over it," said June. This wasn't just for young men. The older men wore sweater vests also.

Something else that men had, like they have now, were razors. It seems that razors started out as sharp metal types with very short handles. Of course, that was when it actually became a razor like those we have now, not when they used a knife-like razor. Also, as the years went on, the handle got longer and the case changed too. After a while there were plastic cases. "Moon blades" for Gillette Razors cost about thirty-one cents for six blades in 1926.

Fashion and History Live On

Every day history is born and some memories live on forever. Although we may never know everything that happened before we were born, we know some things. The same goes for fashion. Fashion changes over the years; trends come and go. Some stay around for a while, and some fade very soon after they are born. Certain trends come back in disguise as new ones. The old fashions become history. Fashions, an important part of history, reflect the values of an era and give designers ideas for new fashions.

I think it is great that we have the chance to research some of the things that happened eighty to a hundred years ago and learn what we want to know. I am glad I had the opportunity to research this type of history and to interview people such as June Redman and Roberta Moellenberg, whom I had not met before this year. When I started my research, I figured that the fashions in Idalia would be behind the times because no television or Internet existed here in the 20's. But I was surprised to find out that they basically wore the same clothes as people in other parts of our country because they had catalogs, newspapers, and magazines. The major differences existed between the work clothes worn by farmers and the "work clothes" of city people.

Sources:
Gail Mansfield, Idalia, Colorado
June Redman, Wray, Colorado
Nolan, Carol. "Ladies Fashion of the 1920's." murrayontravel.com
Roberta Moellenberg, Idalia, Colorado
Sears, Roebuck and Co. *Mid-Summer Sale*. Kansas City, Missouri.
    August 31, 1926.
"The 1920's." www.lousiville.edu/
Wray Museum
"Special Merit School Shoes." Wray, Colorado: *Wray Rattler*, March 27, 1908.

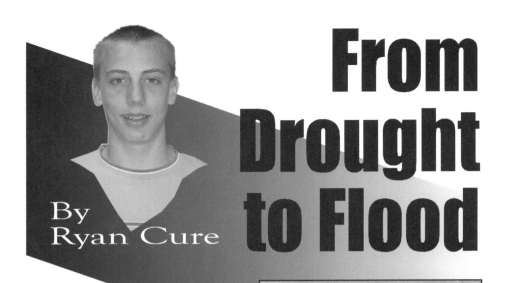

From Drought to Flood

By Ryan Cure

Washed away in the Flood of 1935, the original monument at Beecher Island was erected in 1898 for the soldiers who died in the Battle of Beecher Island. It cost $100. The present monument (above) replaced the original monument of 1898. Photos courtesy of Idalia Community Photo Exhibit.

Imagine being back in the 1930's, probably the most catastrophic time for people in this area for centuries. Dust rolled in, no rain fell, and the heat mounted to torture. The Dust Bowl caused poor vision for everyone in about five states: Kansas, Colorado, Oklahoma, Nebraska, and Texas. Rags sealed windows to keep the dust out. Jars with caps could hardly be stored anywhere without the gritty, sandy dust getting inside. People begged for rain to come, but it just wouldn't fall. Crops only grew to less than half of their normal height, if that. Businesses failed, and citizens had to look for new jobs, but jobs were hard to establish since everyone needed them. Many people just wandered the country looking for work. Many teenagers couldn't find jobs because of their smaller size, leaner strength, and lack of experience. Then finally the Idalia people got rain on May 30, 1935, but this wasn't the kind of rain they wanted. Records show it as the heaviest rain this area has ever had. And, probably, there will never be another one like it.

To uncover this information, I had to use references such as the Internet and books. But the most exciting part of learning about this topic was hearing the stories from actual flood survivors and observers. I would like to thank Burdine Homm, Clarence Lidke, Geneva North, Punk North, and Ward Wiley for telling me their stories and struggles. I would also like to thank Betty and Milton Lampe of St. Francis, Kansas, for The 1935 Republican River Flood, *a book for which they compiled many harrowing flood stories.*

For over five years the citizens of the High Plains had to suffer from the dry weather, the wind, and the heat of the Dust Bowl. I would best describe it as a long, enduring blizzard of dust. But then very suddenly, many people found themselves struggling to get to higher ground during the 1935 Flood. No one could imagine the amount of damage a single storm would accomplish. Or was it two storms? Examiners discovered later that two storms had headed in opposite directions and intersected at a danger zone. This zone happened to be the basin of the Republican and Arickaree Rivers. The

Kansas River nearby caused even more destruction.

After the two storms started, dry stock tanks filled and overflowed as the night rained on. Bridges completely washed away, and many of their parts may now be resting at the bottom of the Gulf of Mexico. Several houses ripped apart as the fearful people living in them floated away with their possessions. A few trees barely within the grasp of would-be survivors provided some aid for their precious lives. The next morning many speculated on the number of lives lost. Twenty? Thirty-Five? Actually, the flood claimed 110 lives from Colorado, Nebraska, and Kansas. Property damage towered as people lost their livestock and many acres of land. Total damage raged at a cost of about fourteen million dollars. (Wilcoxen, p. 37)

The next day, on June 1, people looked for those who could still be alive but endangered. They found that many didn't survive. Some people would just stand by the river and see if anything would come floating past. Once in awhile a house would float by with survivors on top. People on the banks then telephoned for help, and rescuers would get there as soon as possible.

Damage also occurred at Beecher Island, truly an island because the Republican River divided and ran around it. But the flood washed away the entire island. Today only a few buildings stand near this site, northeast of Idalia.

After the flood, trouble still continued. Many trees and wildlife, as well as human lives, were put at risk because the flood caused quicksand in many places near the river. But the flood brought one benefit to this territory: Bonny Dam. This dam, constructed to control future floods, provides a splash full of fun for the few families around here who wish to spend a couple of hours of relaxation, but I do know that this lake isn't worth one life that was lost in the flood.

Stories about the Drought

The drought started around 1930 and didn't end until about 1938. That indicates that the hysteria of getting dust pneumonia went on for eight years. But many say, "The year 1934 was the dirtiest and driest of them all." That year had many dust storms and the least amount of moisture. Burdine Homm of Idalia, Colorado, and Ward Wiley now of Burlington, Colorado, were young in the 1930's, but they recall stories with many factual details. Some dreadful details they will remember forever.

During the drought many people lost cattle because of starvation or disease. In 1930 the government started a program to help save the livelihood of those people who were losing cattle and money, so "government people would go out to those small farms and buy cattle, but only for $13 a head," said Burdine. It wasn't much, but anything helped. They would shoot the cattle but not bury them. The families were still allowed to butcher and use the meat, even though the government was the rightful owner of the cattle. A Corn and Hog Program worked much the same way.

Very poor, jobless people wandered the roads searching for either a job or food. So, not long after, CCC (Civilian Conservation Corps) camps took effect. Homeless people were gathered up to do a variety of jobs for the government, like building roads and digging ditches. Several CCC campers helped construct the Colorado State Fairgrounds.

People regarded themselves as lucky if they had shelter. But when they tried to get some food, they were unlucky after all. Some people planted corn and other vegetables, but Clarence Lidke's family only got the corn to grow about knee high because the land was so dry and dusty due to the drought.

Burdine even remembers how the dust came to her home. "Black clouds of dirt came billowing over the hills and across the land." All of a sudden the easy breathing would be gone, and people had to cover their faces with cloth to keep the dirt out of their lungs; otherwise they could get dust pneumonia. "The women at home would close up their precious items in jars and wrap them with cloth," she said. "Even then those jars would still fill with dirt. Women stuffed their windowsills with cloth to keep out the nasty dirt and sand. But the cloths soon filled with the grit and would have to be replaced. The only good thing that this drought may have caused was that the children sometimes got out of school at noon. But I am sure this was something they didn't prefer to do. They would have to walk home with huge amounts of dust flying in their faces or wait for their parents to pick them up."

A dust storm could easily be compared with the night because it caused such darkness. Fences and buildings were almost always covered with dust. Many people finally gave up and moved to such places as the west coast, mainly because of all the dust but also to look for work. But desperation continued for the people and animals of Idalia.

So desperate was Burdines's father that he cut thistles along the road ditches to use as feed for the cattle. (Most people at that time only had forty to fifty head of cattle, at the most.) But often, that process didn't even help. Many cattle still perished for other reasons, such as the dust. Their lungs would get so full of dirt and mud that they would soon die of dust pneumonia. The wind also blew the dirt right into the cattle's hides. Soon their hides would get so full that their skin could not breathe. After that they would just lie down and die.

A Story about the Flood

The middle years of the drought held the worst misfortune of that time: the 1935 Flood of the Republican River. It seemed that a year's worth of rain came all in one night. Memorial Day of 1935 became a more extensive day of memory than any other Memorial Day.

Ward Wiley tells a story about the flood that includes some shocking detail. Not long before the flood, a family moved in about three-quarters of a mile southwest and downhill of the Wiley home. The day of the flood, water flowed right up against the Wiley's front step; but that meant that their neighbor's home, right in the middle

Ward Wiley, pictured here with his wife Vaudie, witnessed some of the devastating effects of the Flood of 1935. Photo courtesy of Susan Knodel.

A letter to the editor by an Idalia resident published June 3, 1935, by the <u>Wray Rattler</u> (predecessor of the <u>Wray Gazette</u>) explains the horrible damage of the flood. Letter courtesy of Burdine Homm.

EADS LEHMAN WRITES INTERESTING LETTER ABOUT THE FLOODS

1935

Idalia, Monday, June 3.
Wray Rattler, Wray, Colo.,
Friend Frank:

I am just dropping you a few lines in haste. I don't know whether you will get this for several days. We have had no mail since May 30, and all bridges are out on the rivers and no chance to get out to here for several days.

What I told you, that it would be just as wet as it was dry and dusty, has come to pass, but not the way I had it figured. This flood from the west sure put the trimmings on everything. I have investigated the amount of waterfall in different places and I find that 18 inches of water fell at the Louis Fleer place 2 miles east and 4¼ south; and at the Cyral Hoag place on the river by the grove just at the foot of the hill 18 to 20 inches fell; at August Moellenberg's 12½ inches fell, while here on the divide it varied from 4 to 10 inches. My gauge showed 5.25, at Idalia 4¾ inches and so on.

The South Fork of the Republican is the worst place, the damage is in the thousands of dollars. The loss of cattle is terrible. Ed Boden lost 110; Geo. Boden told me he was short 71, and the Waters boys on the old Republican Cattle Co. ranch known as the Bar T, had 2,000 head on the bottom and they have not found very many of them. John Fleer lost some as did Lengels and others on the south side. On the Arickaree, Fox Bros., McCoy, George Conrad and many others have losses.

I have been here a long time but I never saw the full width of the river bottom covered with mud as it is now. Hay land and farm land is covered three to ten feet deep and is ruined for several years to come. The corn planted is either washed out or covered up, and the Lord only knows what is next to happen. Hail stones fell here the size of turkey eggs and were solid with prougs on them. Luckily there was little or no wind.

Memorial day 1935 will be remembered here a long time. I hope such a storm never happens again. We had enough water go to waste for two good crops if distributed at the right time. I'll send you some news when we get service again. The radio is the only chance for news here. If you come out, if you can get across, you will see more than I can tell you. Yours—Eads Lehman.

of the Republican River Valley, was in danger. Later a ten-foot wall of water came down the hill and immediately picked up the neighboring house. Ward watched this incredible event take place right outside of his front window. That house just went floating along; but when it got nearer, Ward saw the father on the roof. Inside were five other members of the family. Just as the house floated in front of Ward's home, it broke and everyone fell in the water. All of them grasped for air and some sort of floating device. Can you imagine the terror a person would feel if this suddenly happened?

Then the search began. The next day searchers found two daughters and a son still conscious, but the remainder of the family wasn't as fortunate. The youngest son was recovered near St. Francis, Kansas. Meanwhile, the mother was found near Benkelman, Nebraska; but the search for her husband continued. Then a second flood rolled by on June 16, though not nearly as harsh as the previous flood. Later, a rancher near St. Francis, while checking his land, accidentally saw a hand sticking out of the quicksand. The hand belonged to the father of the family.

Other Flood Stories from Nearby Areas

A book entitled *The 1935 Republican River Flood* contains other flood stories, compiled by Betty and Milton Lampe of St. Francis, Kansas.

One of the stories tells of Mr. Otto Ludwig's family. This family lived in a valley near the Republican River close to St. Francis. During the flood, the family got in some serious trouble when they tried to reach higher ground. While on their journey to safety in the water, many snakes surrounded them, since these and other animals were also trying to reach safety. The whole family, though, luckily managed to avoid them.

Another story from the Lampes' book is told by Vivien (nee Hurlock) Horwege of St. Francis. Vivien planned to attend summer school with a friend on May 31. But as one can guess, that had to be delayed because of the flood. Trapped, Vivien and her family didn't know how to reach safety. All of a sudden they saw a small airplane come out of the clouds. The plane circled their home, and then a note fastened to a rock fell from the plane. It read, "If you can get to the river by the Hol family home, you can get across the river by boat." It also said that Vivien's friend was still waiting in town for her to go to summer school. The family hurried to the river and, sure enough, a rowboat waited there to take them across. For Vivien, "The small plane and its welcome message were like a message from heaven."

A story about the quick, heroic actions of a Hereford bull is also recorded in Lampes' book. A herd of cows and heifers along with some bulls got caught up in the river as they tried to swim to safety.

Bystanders observe and discuss the destruction of the Flood of 1935. These tracks were derailed but strangely unbroken. Photo courtesy of the Wray Museum.

A Hereford bull reached the shore and immediately looked to make sure the rest of the herd had no troubles in the water. But a small heifer struggled in the water, due to a strong current. The bull saw the victim and injected into the raging water. He made it to the struggling heifer, and it appeared that the bull showed the heifer a safe way through the water. The many spectators watching said they could easily tell that the bull truly tried to save the heifer.

A fascinating story of a family pure of luck concerns the Webb Scheller family of St. Francis, told by Shirley Scheller Achabal. Webb and his wife Rose had three children: Sam, age 8; Shirley, (age not given); and Billy, age 4. On the evening of the flood, Sam had gone to visit his aunt and uncle. About ten o'clock that night no one in the Scheller family knew how badly the storm raged. Then Rose looked out the door to see an illuminating flash of lightning. Water! That would be a good explanation of what she saw in that slight second. The whole family then immediately started to bail buckets full of water out of the house.

The next morning everyone saw the damage of the flood. "What a sight it was!!" Then they discovered a granary floating straight toward their cow shed. The granary collided into the shed, which housed milk cows and a Shetland pony with its colt. The animals were all swept away by the flood waters. "We never expected to see them again," wrote Shirley. Then Shirley's father and his hired man went to check on the horses in the barn. The water nearly drowned the horses, as it had risen up to their backs. But the two men could do nothing, so they went back to the house. They said there were snakes and many other objects in the water.

Next the family decided that they needed to leave their home and go to higher land, but they would have to go through the wild water. Shirley's father put four-year-old Billy on the hired man's back and everyone linked hands. Together they made it to the barn. The father and Shirley rode on the mare, while the others walked behind the horse. On their way to safety, they heard a loud outcry for help from a young boy clinging to a tree. Shirley's father told him that help would soon be on the way. The family continued through the water, but the horse fell into an invisible hole. The horse, Shirley,

Railroads were one of many damages of the greedy flood. Photo courtesy of the Wray Museum.

Some people used one of the sturdier bridges that survived the harsh night of May 30, 1935, to look for possible survivors or bodies in the water. Photo courtesy of the Wray Museum.

and her father "went out of sight." Luckily the father hung on and was able to make a grab for Shirley. The other three were now aware of the hole and knew to go around. Everyone soon "MADE IT OUT TO DRY LAND!!"

Ten to fifteen men, informed about the struggling boy, went on the mission to save him. By the time they got there, the water had washed out the tree and thrown the boy out into the flood. Fortunately, he grabbed a piece of sturdy machinery lodged in the water and hung on until he was rescued.

Later that evening, the Scheller's Shetland pony and its colt were found, alive, about three to four miles away from the Scheller home. "It was a miracle how she was able to keep the little one with her all the way to where they finally lodged," said Shirley Scheller.

Conclusion

One has to conclude that the most dreadful decade for our area was truly the 1930's. The stories and memories will be preserved; and the people lost during those years, whether they perished by dust pneumonia or were swept away by the flood, will be remembered. Droughts still take place, but in the United States few die from them as we now have more technology. Floods also occur often, but dams help prevent some of their danger. Thankfully we have Bonny Dam built right next door. The 1930's will truly be remembered by the people in our tri-state area.

Sources:
Burdine Homm, Burlington, Colorado
Clarence Lidke, Idalia, Colorado
Punk and Geneva North, Wray, Colorado
Ward Wiley, Burlington, Colorado
"Bluff to Bluff"
    http://www.esull.org/projects/NatDisaster/floods/Flood/BB_Chapter29/
    bluff_to_bluff_chapter_29/html
Lampe, Betty and Milton. *The 1935 Republican River Flood.* St. Francis, Kansas:
    Cheyenne County Historical Society and Independent Printing, 2001.
Wilcoxen, Tommie. "The Flood of 1935." *Idalia Centennial 1887-1987.*
Wilmot, Marlene (nee Harvey). *Bluff-to-Bluff.* Greeley, Colorado: Wilmot Venters,
    Inc., 1995.

The Start of Irrigation in Yuma County

By
German Penzing

Burdine and Howard Homm live down by the Bar T Ranch southwest of Idalia. Photo courtesy of Howard and Burdine Homm.

The Republican River has provided water supply for irrigation in the Idalia area since the 1880's. Writing Lab photo.

This topic was not a hard choice for me. Ken Penzing, my father and an agronomist, knows a lot about plants and irrigation. Therefore, he could help me with this appealing topic. Farming is what small towns like Idalia are all about, and irrigation plays the biggest role in that. I wanted to put myself into this kind of lifestyle, that isn't really discussed very much, and learn how people really made it work.

I rrigation, a backbreaking job in the old days, had to be done by some people to earn a living. Out here people didn't have as many choices as we do now. Farming and ranching probably provided the two biggest jobs; and throughout the years, the technology of irrigation has definitely improved. Originally, rainfall moisture kept crops growing as healthy as possible. Then irrigating out of the river changed to deep well irrigation here in Yuma County, and now to irrigating by using ponds, ditches, and sprinklers. We would not have economized and furthered ourselves as much if we wouldn't have sprinklers and other such devices.

Burdine Richards has lived near Idalia all her life and is now married to Howard Homm. She recalls the "good old days" when they still had to use horses to make irrigation ditches and shovels to fix the rows every day. Burdine, a very energetic lady filled with many splendid stories of her younger days says, "Some irrigation ditches that were adjudicated are still working, but the 1935 Flood destroyed others. This flood amazingly changed our lives and how well people adapted to their problems."

Irrigating Out of the River

The first water rights of people in Yuma County allowed them to irrigate out of a river. According to Burdine, "Irrigation started around here in the 1880's by using ditches." Some of these ditches located on the Republican River include Tuttle Ditch at the

McArther, the Garfield Ditch on the Bar T, and the Republican Ditch and the Ragan Ditch on Homm Ranches, which were adjudicated. In 1883 a number of ditches were located on the Republican River. An adjudicated ditch is "an inter-county drainage ditch maintained under the jurisdiction of the circuit court" (Herren and Donahue).

"In order to get adjudication, a person from the State Department would come out to your land and see where you wanted to do your irrigation and check how much water you would be taking out of the river," said Howard, husband of Burdine. "One could only take so many cubic feet per acre of water, so people down the river would also have their fair share of water. If you were taking out more water than you were supposed to, then all you would have to do is slow down the amount of water your headgate was taking out."

The people owned these ditches and sometimes several people owned and used them together. For example, the Republican Ditch was built and owned by the Bar T Ranch. "Later some of the Bar T was sold to William and John Richards, my grandfather and dad who bought the Republican ditch along with the land that is irrigated," said Burdine. After Howard and Burdine married, they bought the Ragan Place from the Ragan Estate along with the Ragan Ditch. They still own the ditches and use them today. Howard and Burdine are retired and still live on the ranches.

The Process of Making a Ditch

In the 1880's farmers only had horses to pull machinery, so they needed many horses to build ditches, especially to pull scrapers. Scrapers were large steel pans or scoops used to excavate a surface. Whoever ran the scraper had to be good because he could let the scraper get in too deep, and then the scraper would either tip over or would build up so much sand that the horse would not be able to pull it. Many of the neighbors got together and helped each other by combining their horses and machinery. If one would try to dig a

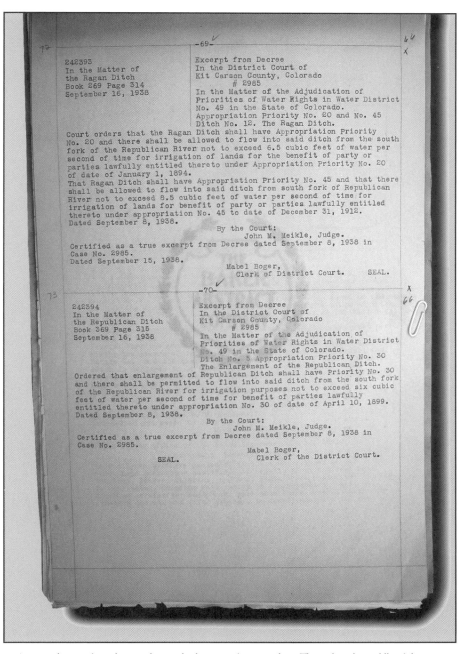

-69-

242393
In the Matter of
the Ragan Ditch
Book 269 Page 314
September 16, 1938

Excerpt from Decree
In the District Court of
Kit Carson County, Colorado
2985
In the Matter of the Adjudication of
Priorities of Water Rights in Water District
No. 49 in the State of Colorado.
Appropriation Priority No. 20 and No. 45
Ditch No. 12. The Ragan Ditch.

Court orders that the Ragan Ditch shall have Appropriation Priority
No. 20 and there shall be allowed to flow into said ditch from the south
fork of the Republican River not to exceed 6.5 cubic feet of water per
second of time for irrigation of lands for the benefit of party or
parties lawfully entitled thereto under Appropriation Priority No. 20
of date of January 1, 1894.
That Ragan Ditch shall have Appropriation Priority No. 45 and that there
shall be allowed to flow into said ditch from south fork of Republican
River not to exceed 8.5 cubic feet of water per second of time for
irrigation of lands for benefit of party or parties lawfully entitled
thereto under appropriation No. 45 to date of December 31, 1912.
Dated September 8, 1938.

By the Court:
John M. Meikle, Judge.

Certified as a true excerpt from Decree dated September 8, 1938 in
Case No. 2985.
Dated September 15, 1938.

Mabel Boger,
Clerk of District Court.   SEAL.

-70-

242394
In the Matter of
the Republican Ditch
Book 369 Page 315
September 16, 1938

Excerpt from Decree
In the District Court of
Kit Carson County, Colorado
2985
In the Matter of the Adjudication of
Priorities of Water Rights in Water District
No. 49 in the State of Colorado.
Ditch No. 5 Appropriation Priority No. 30
The Enlargement of the Republican Ditch.

Ordered that enlargement of Republican Ditch shall have Priority No. 30
and there shall be permitted to flow into said ditch from the south fork
of the Republican River for irrigation purposes not to exceed six cubic
feet of water per second of time for benefit of parties lawfully
entitled thereto under appropriation No. 30 of date of April 10, 1899.
Dated September 8, 1938.

By the Court:
John M. Meikle, Judge.

Certified as a true excerpt from Decree dated September 8, 1938 in
Case No. 2985.

SEAL.

Mabel Boger,
Clerk of the District Court.

An actual copy of an abstract shows adjudication of water rights. The seal in the middle of the page indicates the significance of the Ragan and Republican Ditches.
Abstract courtesy of Howard and Burdine Homm.

ditch by himself, it would take much longer and be almost impossible to do. Astonishingly, people always can work together and help each other, a special thing that occurs often in small communities.

Making ditches would take a lot of work; so setting up all the ditches would take most of the early spring to get things ready by April, when the ground is thawed and ready to work. When someone had enough water running into a ditch, he would use a shovel to cut little rows leading from the ditch to let the water run out into a field, a never-ending job. Every day someone would have to walk up and down the field to fix the rows because the water would wash them out.

Burdine also tells how the beavers would always ruin everything. At one time, no trees grew down in the river bottoms; but after the 1935 Flood, trees just started to multiply. She now thinks that we will again lose the trees because of the beavers. Ah, yes, the beavers. Such cute little animals to some people, but a nuisance to the devoted farmers. Burdine says, "The beavers only take the young, tasty trees and leave the old ones to die. That would cause the young trees to die; and with the old ones already dead, the river would dry up." (Trees provide shade to hold moisture.) Farmers really hated the creatures because they also dammed up the river with the trees and the water didn't flow down to the ditches. But beavers did not present the only problem.

The 1935 Flood caused other problems for some of the farmers. It ruined many of their crops because it carried sand into the fields. Also, many of them lost their headgates and didn't have money to get them back. Only a few fortunate ones got them back. This loss of headgates put many families in danger of not having crops to provide income. Some of the headgates that were lost in the flood included those belonging to Davis, Mace, Garfield, Ireland, and Chase. They never got their headgates relocated, so most had to find other jobs.

What does a headgate do? It amounts to being a structure that dams up the river and converts it out. It is made out of concrete with a metal sheet that can be moved up and down in the concrete. That metal sheet regulates the amount of water coming out of the river and into a ditch or a pond.

The ditches that amazingly made it through the flood included the Tuttle, Ragan, Republican, Fleer, Boden, and Lengel Ditches. These ditches, the ones that relocated, are still being used today. "Relocating a headgate meant someone had to go back to the court to get his water rights back. It was as if he got a new water right because the headgate had to be replaced and relocated to another place. Even if one had to move his headgate an inch, he had to get permission," said Burdine.

Siphon Tubes

After all of this, people looked for a better and more efficient way to run water to their crops. New advancements in technology brought the usage of siphon tubes that were about one and one-half to two inches in diameter. Farmers would put one end of these tubes down into the water and cover the other end with their hand to create a type of suction to allow the water to flow out through the tube. According to Howard, "You have to be as good at starting si-

Since technology has advanced, old siphon tubes now lie in a heaping pile in an old pickup bed. These tubes once indicated the start of new ideas in irrigation. Writing Lab photo.

phon tubes as you can walk."

One day I went down to the river with Colt Strick, a high school friend, to try our luck at getting siphon tubes to work. Being the first one to try, I figured it would be an easy task that I could easily handle. I used the method Howard taught me. Covering one end of the tube to create a suction to pull water into the tube, I tried numerous times; but only a dribble of water came out, when I was lucky. Other times I would get water to splash out the end, but nothing more ever seemed to come. It's hard to believe people could start those siphon tubes just as fast as they could walk.

Next Colt, the cowboy, gave it his best try with a different idea. He put his mouth on the end of the tube and tried to suck the water into a flow, but he only swallowed a mouthful of cold, dirty, river water. Talk about funny! Colt figured that since the tube had the name "siphon" with it, he would siphon it out with his mouth. Sad to admit, but we will never do well at that job.

These tubes saved a lot of time because people didn't have to redo the ditch rows everyday, and the tubes provided more water supply than rows of ditches that always washed out. Today a few people still use siphon tubes to get their water running, but another invention provided new possibilities for greater water supply.

Deep Well Irrigation

Deep well irrigation got water from underground in new and abundant ways. A man named Ernest Romkee provided possibilities for that type of irrigation here in Yuma County. The farm where it all started lies about fifteen miles west and a few miles south of Idalia, Colorado. But this grand, new technology also created new conflicts. The water flow from the river would short out because of these wells. Burdine said, "Out of the seventy-five years I have lived here, a few years ago the river went dry for the first time." She and other people believe that the irrigation pumps caused it to go dry. But, surprisingly, the river only ran out of water once in seventy-five years!! Burdine explained that the river came back because of the springs that come up from the ground. Howard said, "If you were to walk out to the middle of the river and wade around for a while, you would feel cold spots in the river, indicating the cold-water springs coming up from the ground."

Sprinklers

When I asked Burdine and Howard what they considered the latest irrigation improvement brought on by technology, they both said, "Sprinklers." Sprinklers appeared around the early 1960's, but the first time the Homms got one was in 1968. "I am already starting to worry about not having sprinkler systems in the near future," said Burdine. She thinks that sprinklers may become obsolete. "I have a bad feeling that soon we just won't have them anymore," she said.

A sprinkler system sits waiting for the ground to thaw before it can be used to water the crops. Sprinklers are the newest form of irrigation. Writing Lab photo.

"The way we farm out here in the Great Plains is extremely different than in the Midwest. In the Midwest, they depend strictly on rainfall because they always have rain there and don't need to have an irrigation system. We may have it rougher out here, but we have our own way to enjoy it."

How do sprinkler systems work? Cy Homm, grandson of Burdine and Howard, said the systems work by having water pumped out of a well or pond into a sprinkler. A type of low energy system requires the sprinklers to be on a set time. The first set of wheels doesn't run at the same speed as the outer set of wheels. The ones on the outside have to go faster in order to set the pace for the inner ones, as they rotate in a circle.

One still has to get water rights from the state, but he is allowed only so many cubic feet of water per second. Sprinklers are more efficient than siphon tubes because the tubes always run over. Also, one has to always check the tubes because they can get air pockets in them, which would stop the water flow and cause a row of crops not to get watered. Sprinklers can be set for running and stopping times; and presto, a consistent flow of water goes to every bit of the crops on schedule.

I really doubt that sprinklers will become obsolete; they are still very consistent and helpful. The only way that a sprinkler would be shut down would be if a well dried up. But that is possible and a real concern now that our Ogallala Aquifer is being depleted.

The Future

Finally we ask ourselves, "What does the future hold for us with irrigation?" Many people gave the same answer. My father Ken Penzing, agronomist for the Cure Brothers, told me that maybe the future will have to go back to dryland farming. "They will make better hybrids that can tolerate not having as much water," he said. With all of the great technology we have, we should be able to develop a seed that can depend mostly on rainfall moisture.

Howard said the same thing that my father said, "There is nothing to do but go back to dryland farming." He explains how "there is a big crisis between Kansas, Nebraska, and Colorado's use of water." He says, "Nebraska and Kansas are complaining because Colorado is supposedly taking too much water from the Ogallala Aquifer." The outcome of that debate will determine whether we will have enough water in the future.

But as powerful as we think we are, I don't think we could create water with technology. We will probably go back through the same cycle we started. The water may not be gone forever but will need many years to build up before irrigation starts again.

All we can do now is farm with the water that we have and see how the aquifer problem develops. Technology amazingly took us from dryland farming, to the usage of siphon tubes, and now to using sprinklers. I hope that we don't run out of water soon because farming on the High Plains depends on water.

Sources:
Burdine and Howard Homm, Idalia, Colorado
Cy Homm, Idalia, Colorado
Ken Penzing, Idalia, Colorado
Herren, Ray V. and Roy L. Donahue. "Judicial Ditch." *The Agriculture Dictionary.* Albany, NY: Delmar Publishers, 1991.

Give Me the Country Life

By
Whitney Weyerman

William Gerber, father of Marie Weyerman, pulled his old harvesting equipment with a tractor (here & below) before he purchased a self-propelled combine. Photos courtesy of Marie Weyerman.

Lynn Weyerman now uses this 1980 Model 750 Massey Ferguson combine to harvest his wheat and corn. Writing Lab photo.

At the beginning of this year in Writing Lab, I was psyched because I like to write. Now I have my final story on farming. I greatly enjoyed gathering information for my article and interviewing Gramma and Daddy. Since they have farmed and lived in this area all of their lives, I knew they would be very reliable sources for my story. The best part of interviewing Gramma is that she is full of information, and she told me everything that she knew with great detail. When I interviewed my father, it was originally for an English class essay; so Dad told me about his childhood memories of harvest time. I would like to thank Daddy and Gramma for taking time to let me interview them. I love ya! As for the rest of y'all, I hope to enlighten you a little on the aspects of farming from the past into the present.

Harvesting with Four Generations

Gramma Marie Weyerman of rural Idalia has lived on a farm all her life. Now eighty years old, she has lots of wonderful information and memories about farming. As a little girl, Marie Gerber would help her father William Gerber with the farm work and chores. They would get up early in the morning and start their long day by milking cows and then heading in for breakfast. Later they would feed the chickens, pigs, horses, and cows. And then they would start on the rest of their farming work. The little girl would also help her mother fix dinner, the noon meal. Except during harvesting season, her father and siblings would come in to eat dinner, take a little nap, and then go out to the field to continue whatever they were doing.

Then in 1945 Marie married Jerry Ralph Weyerman and they had four children, including my father, Lynn Wayne Weyerman. When Dad was just a little squirt, he would help harvest the wheat crop in July. Dad drove the tractor that pulled the combine. He was told to watch his driving and watch Grandpa's signals. Grandpa would use all sorts of funny hand signals for what he wanted Dad to do. He would move his finger around in a circle to mean "go faster." He would move his hand side to side which meant "slow down." Raising his hand and lowering it meant "stop!" And he would run his finger across his throat, which meant "kill it" or "shut it off." Now my father uses these hand signals. I am usually very confused by them, but I am beginning to understand. Dad said that if he did not pay attention to what Grandpa wanted, Grandpa would throw wheat at him.

At noon, Gramma would bring the harvest dinner to the field. Dad said, "Gramma would usually pack me an extra piece of chocolate cake that I would eat in the afternoon for a snack." He couldn't eat and drive at the same time, so he would place the cake on top of the plastic sack and put both of those on top of the toolbox. He said, "I probably ate more chaff and dirt than cake, but it tasted good because I got hungry."

Their water jugs consisted of glass vinegar jugs covered with burlap sacks. Dad said, "The water jugs would get some green, slimy, mossy stuff in the bottom of the jug, but your Grandpa would take some gravel and throw it in the jug with some water and shake it around. It would knock all of the slimy stuff out of the jug, and then we would use the water jug right after we got all of the slimy stuff out of it." No offense to them, but that seems just a little nasty. Dad also said, "If we wet the burlap, it would keep the water colder much longer."

Dad drove the tractor until they got a self-propelled combine, when he was fifteen or sixteen years old. Moving from field to field proved to be a large challenge back then. They had to unhook all of the implements and put them on a trailer to haul them down the road. (Now farmers just drive everything down the road.) They would go to the field at about 8:00 in the morning to fuel and grease the tractor and combine. Then they would start cutting about 9:00 or when the wheat was dry enough to cut. Once they started cutting, they wouldn't stop until dark.

When Grandpa got the self-propelled combine, it didn't have an air conditioner, radio, or any of the modern luxuries we have now. The combine didn't even have a cab. And, even though a self-propelled combine only took one person to drive it, Dad did not get cut from a job. He drove the combine and Grandpa drove the truck to haul the wheat. Harvesting today is much better than when my dad was young because we have conveniences like cabs and air conditioners.

In our part of Colorado, crops really haven't varied much over the years. We may have gone from non-Roundup ready corn to Roundup ready corn (Roundup kills weeds but not corn), but the basic types of crops that we grow haven't changed much. They used to grow wheat, corn, and alfalfa. And they would grow beans, tomatoes, and some other vegetables in their gardens. Also corn, millet, and cane were needed because that was about all that the cattle would eat. We still basically grow the same things, with a few exceptions. Today sugar beets, beans, and potatoes aren't just meant for a garden; they have become cash crops. Today farmers haul a harvested crop to Co-op for storage until the owners get ready to sell it. Earlier, farmers would basically just keep all of the crops for their cows and livestock to eat.

Working with Livestock

Cows were milked twice a day, in the early morning and in the evening before dark. First Gramma and her family would have to go out into the pasture and round up the cows. Then they would bring them into the corrals and the barn. Right before they milked the cows, they would give them hay or grain to eat, so the cows could eat as they were getting milked.

When milk cows had calves, the calves were not allowed to run with the milk cows. Gramma would help feed the calves separately after they milked the cows. Then she ran the extra milk through a separator. A separator is a machine that separates the cream from the milk with a series of disks. Then they would sell the cream. Gramma would keep the milk to drink, have with cereal, cook with, and give a little to the cats. But, in addition to doing these daily chores, farmers and ranchers today must take care of their livestock all year long.

After Gramma Marie Weyerman helped milked their cows, this separator used a series of discs to separate the cream from the milk. Writing Lab photo.

Marie and Jerry (her husband) Weyerman used cream cans to transport to town the cream they wished to sell.
Writing Lab photo

In the summer, cattle graze in pastures, but by midwinter the grass dies down and new feed must be found. In earlier times farmers and ranchers used horses to move cows to and from fields of corn stalks. (Corn dropped behind during harvesting and the stalks themselves provide lots of nourishment for cattle.) Now we use pickups, four-wheelers, and sometimes horses to move cattle. People also run behind and beside the cows on foot. Running along and behind isn't that bad of a job until one is running in a ditch and steps in a big hole, or he is running along the road behind the cows and steps in a big cow pie! (That stinks terribly bad!)

When fields run out of corn stalks, farmers move the cattle home and feed them in the corrals. Feed consists of ensilage, ground hay, and protein. Water is provided by a stock tank, but someone usually

A cow chute and alleys are often used in the branding of cattle. A calf cradle is smaller than a chute and can be moved into a cradle position for castrating a calf. Writing Lab photo.

A black cow on the Weyerman farm stands near some old machinery that she uses for a scratching tool. Writing Lab photo.

has to break and throw the ice off of it every winter morning.

Also in the winter, blizzards challenge farmers, ranchers, and live-stock. It is very wise to have livestock close to home during the winter. It is also a good idea to have a building or shelter for the animals. During blizzards cattle tend to wander, and sometimes they wander away from where they are supposed to be. Blizzards can also be very dangerous because of the frigid temperatures and the blinding and blowing snow.

Spring is a busy time of the year. Cows will usually calve from the middle of March through the end of May. If cows seem to have trouble calving, farmers have to pull their calves. It always seems that cows have trouble calving when it is dark and cold outside. But not much can really be done about that. To pull a calf, one must use a device called a calf puller. The calf puller is attached to the front two feet of a calf, while still unborn. Then to operate the calf puller, one pulls a handle that will roll up a cable that does the pulling of the calf, therefore the name "calf puller."

Another job in the spring is branding and working calves. Still today, some men wrestle the calves down to brand them and work them. But chutes and alleys can confine them so the work is sometimes easier to do. Calves will not always cooperate, and that makes the job twice as hard as it really needs to be. On our farm, when we load calves to take to the sale barn, we seem to always have one of our calves break its leg. Now it's only happened twice, but we hope we haven't started a tradition.

Animals do not come with a warranty or guarantee, and many things can go wrong. Cattle will bloat or get scours, foot rot, black leg, scabies, pneumonia, pink eye, and red nose, just to name a few conditions or diseases. Vaccines help prevent these problems, but livestock constantly require close care and surveillance. On the other hand, they also provide meat, dairy products, and a source of income.

Gramma's and My Thoughts on Farming

Whitney: Today we can do most of our farm work with tractors. Before tractors and sophisticated machinery, farmers had to do all of their work by hand. I think we owe most of today's success in the farming industry to advances in technology.

* * * * *

Whitney: Farmers and ranchers raise basically the same animals that they did a long time ago. Then they had cattle, milk cows, horses, donkeys, pigs, mules, and chickens. Now we still have basically the same farm animals, but some people also own ducks, geese, goats, sheep, turkeys, ostriches, emus, and even llamas.

* * * * *

Gramma: We would butcher our pigs, chickens, turkeys, and cattle for food for ourselves. We wouldn't always just sell them. We would gather the chicken eggs, but leave some so the hens could have baby chicks. We would butcher the chickens and turkeys for Christmas dinner but also eat wild game that we hunted. We had deer, rabbits, ducks, geese, and pheasants. Turkeys, pheasants,

A group of threshers including Marie (Gerber) Weyerman and her brother Fritz Gerber (front row with light shirts and dark pants) line up after a long day's work. Photo courtesy of Marie Weyerman.

William Gerber, father of Marie Weyerman, used a Wiseman thresher for their wheat crop on the Gerber farm. Threshing machines were used before combines were invented. Photo courtesy of Marie Weyerman.

Fritz Gerber, brother of Marie Weyerman, used this tractor for many farm operations. Photo courtesy of Marie Weyerman.

Lynn Weyerman's bulk bin stores corn for winter feeding of cattle. Writing Lab photo.

ducks, geese, and chickens are all basically the same type of food.

* * * * *

Whitney: Many people stereotype farm people. The stereotype is that farm people have no manners, eat unusual road kill stews, are uneducated beings, and have no clue as to what the real world is like. I hate to break this news to them, but they're WRONG!! I believe that farm people have a better perspective as to what the real world is like. I believe this because we actually work for our own living and don't depend on a job with hours and a job description set by someone else.

* * * * *

Gramma: Living and working on a farm has proven to be challenging because how your crops and animals do depends on your weather conditions. If you don't have rain your crops won't grow, and the grass in your pastures for your cows won't grow. If the grass doesn't grow, then your cows won't have anything to eat over the summer.

* * * * *

Gramma: Back in the early years everything was about taking it one day at a time. People would very rarely look forward into the future. But now days we look into the future far too much and far too often.

* * * * *

Whitney: Lots of people have the assumption that farm people always have beef and potatoes for meals. But that's not true. We eat many things. We have chicken, turkey, ham, corn, peas, green beans, potatoes, and lots of other vegetables.

* * * * *

Gramma: I asked my Gramma about cow dogs, and this is what she had to say. "Yup, we always had cow dogs. They would always make working and moving cows easier. The cows must have known that when the dogs were behind them and if they didn't go, they were going to get their hocks bitten."

* * * * *

Gramma: The 1970's brought hard times for many farmers. Extreme drought conditions caused many people to sell their farms. When cleaning house, washing dishes, and farming are basically all you know, it would be very hard to sell your farm and move on to a new life.

* * * * *

I have only lived on a farm my short sixteen years, but I have to say that I love it. I really do believe that people who live in a rural area have good lives. When you live near a little town like Idalia, people know you. Most of them have known you since you were a baby. Living here gives you a family, other than the people to whom you are actually related.

If you had to choose to live in Idalia or in a city like Boulder, Denver, or even Los Angeles, what would you choose? I like to go to the big cities to shop once in a while, but after a few days I want to go home. Big cities are not for me; smaller cities and rural areas are for me. People think that for a vacation they need to go to a big city and do sight seeing, shopping, and everything else that can be done in the city. But if I was used to a big city, I would want to come out here to Idalia or other rural area for a calm, relaxing, and peaceful vacation. Think about it, breathing in pollution to see a big city or fresh country air for refreshing peace and quiet. Give me the country life!

Sources:
Lynn Weyerman, Idalia, Colorado
Marie Weyerman, Idalia, Colorado

Smoking Brands

By
Colt Strick

The S and reverse C over C brand (front left and Diagram D) currently belongs to Mike, Colt, and Cody Strick. The two prominent irons in the photo are used together to make the one brand. The family's original brand, Lazy V over Y (far left), now belongs to James Strick of Kirk. Writing Lab photo.

Introduction

I have always considered myself a cowboy. As a young lad I carried a kiddy rope everywhere, especially while traveling to rodeos with my aunt, uncle, and their two children. They owned a western wear store near Denver and had me decked out in the finest western apparel. My wardrobe has always consisted of a cowboy hat and a pair of boots. Riding horses comes naturally to me, but then I've been in the saddle practically since birth. Breaking colts became my job at the tender age of fourteen, and it has been my job and a hobby ever since. My childhood was great, but it was focused mostly in the Denver area and there "ain't" many cows there. "Cow-ology" pretty well began for me in 1998 when Idalia became my new home. Thanks to some wonderful help from good people, good horses, and parents that back me one-hundred percent no matter what, I am becoming a real cowboy. I thank all those who have "larned me good"; and I am grateful for all the bad "broncs," hard dives, and especially those wild, old, mossy-horned cows that have been dealt with in creating one more of the dying breed.

Overture

Warm, late spring weather carries a little gusty breeze blowing in from the northeast. The breeze brings a slight chill off the dewy ground as the cattle graze quietly in the rolling, high plains pasture. Down by the ranch house, the racket of diesel engines, rattling stock trailers, and many barking dogs kill the peaceful morning. The local cowboys show up one and two at a time; and, of course, they all have their dogs and a good saddle horse or two. After quick cups of pure cowboy coffee, they saddle their horses and mount up. One or two bring their dogs, but the rest of the barking frenzy stay in the yard. The cowboys set out across the pasture at a trot, and the smell of wet sage and warming sod gives each a feeling of purity. Every cowboy awaits this time of year, and it has finally arrived! Slowly the cowboys begin rounding up the cattle and bringing the

Some cowboys on the Fox Brothers Ranch use a primitive squeeze chute to work cattle in the late 1890's. Photo courtesy of Wray Museum.

The alley behind the chute at the Fox Brothers Ranch holds cattle that will soon be pushed into the chute. Photo courtesy of Wray Museum.

entire herd together at the windmill.

Then after watering their ponies and tightening their cinches, the cowboys begin driving the cattle back toward the corrals. Once the cattle are in a corral, a couple of pards who work well together swap their okay horses for their good cutters. Approaching the herd slowly, they begin sorting the calves from the cows. The initial slow speed soon turns to a quick-paced cutting match that leaves dust swirling about the corrals. Cowboys sit atop their mounts, straight and tall like kings on thrones. But the quick movements of the horses stir more dust into the chalky air as they dart to and fro, stopping the cattle from any foolish moves that would bungle the operation. Cows separated from their calves are moved to a working pen with a chute and the calves are pushed into the roping pen.

Then a couple of the older cowmen start to back pour the cows for lice and other vermin. Back pouring rids cattle of parasites that can cause diseases in a herd or cause cattle to lose weight because of stress. To back pour, ranchers use chemicals that kill the bugs and pour doses of it along the backs of the cattle. The alternative to pouring is dipping. To dip cattle, they run them into a trough, also called a dipping vat, full of similar chemicals and bath them in that. Vaccines and sterile scalpels are readied while the irons are heating. Each cowboy has a certain job to do, and each knows his place. One will brand, one will castrate, and another will de-horn. Others (maybe women) will rope, some will mug, and a few will vaccinate. I have seen women do all of the jobs on a crew except mug, and I have no doubt they can do that as well.

The branding process itself starts with the roper. He rides his horse into the pen of calves, ropes the two back feet of a choice critter, and dallies his rope to his saddle horn. He then rides out of the pen, dragging a bawling calf by its back feet. It is important that the roper catches both legs in order to contribute to the safety and convenience of the ground crew. The muggers' job follows next. The struggling calf gets thrown down on the ground, with the side to be branded turned upward. One mugger then grabs the hind legs, and the other sits up on the head and shoulders of the calf to hold it down. The man on the hind feet takes off the cowboy's rope so he can go catch another calf. Mugging is serious business because the rest of the ground crews' safety depends on how it's done. Calves will kick and try to butt their heads, and the muggers have to prevent this, no easy task with a four-month-old calf. After the calf is mugged down, the "brander" comes with cherry hot irons to scorch its hide with the design designated to that ranch or owner. This action shows the ownership of that critter.

Every brand in Colorado is registered with the state brand office. To further prove ownership, a beef may also have an ear notched. (This is also registered with the brand office.) Branding probably burns the calves a little, but it is nothing too serious. It mainly chars the thick, tough hide that covers the more tender skin.

Next, the castrator removes the bull calves' testicles, thus making them steers and rendering them useless for breeding. This prevents inbreeding and also makes the calves easier to sell at weaning time. Many calves have nubs of horns, and these are removed with a "spoon," a tool with one sharp edge for digging down under the "button" and getting it by the "roots." Nowadays calves are also vaccinated at branding time to prevent herd diseases and sicknesses that may cause weight loss and death during the grazing season. Calves raise much noise and commotion during this entire process, not because of the pain but because of these frightening new experiences that involve so many people.

Diagram A

Diagram B

Diagram C

Diagram D

Diagram E

Entr'acte

Branding is probably one of the oldest practices in the world. The Egyptians branded stock and their slaves, and the Spanish brought branding to the Americas. Horse and cattle branding provide the largest example of branding still practiced today. Brands should be read from top to bottom and left to right, as well as outside in. Some brand examples include the Bar T (Diagram A), Seven Slash (Diagram B), and the Lazy TH (Diagram C). The Bar T is a local ranch owned by Ronald and Gretchen Brittain, and the Lazy TH belongs to Larry Homm, south of Idalia. The Seven Slash is an old brand from a ranch on the Arickaree River. Brands often reflect the owner's character or something unique about his spread (ranch); for example, our brand (Diagram D) represents "Strick, Colt and Cody," for my sister and I. Of course, I am the reversed C.

Typically four different categories of brands exist. A monogram features one design all connected, like the Lazy TH. A phonogram has two or more letters not connected. This is a very common style, like our S and reverse C over

C. The pictograph has letters, numbers, or symbols representing a picture like the Box T (Diagram E), and a word story brand tells a story. A Time-Life book entitled *The Cowboys*, from the Old West series, gives an example of a word story told through a brand. It says a man was a fool to raise cattle in Texas, and later that became that man's brand: FOOL.

Cattle can be branded on the hips, ribs, jaws, or sides of their bodies. The different symbols used in brands (such as combinations of letters, slashes, bars, rafters, and quarter circles) make a list too long to include. Brands help prevent rustling (stealing) of stock. However, a rustler can easily convert some brands into a new brand by adding a bar or some other symbol to the original, but our justice system levies severe fines or imprisonment against rustlers who are prosecuted.

Some Cowboy Lore

Late in the spring of 2001 Cy Homm, who lives south of Idalia, Colorado; his brother Bob of Burlington, Colorado; and I drove to Castle Rock, Colorado, just to brand calves. The Homms have been branding for a ranch down there for quite a few years, and they invited me to go along to enjoy the fun and to experience a branding of this magnitude. Because of their experience and because they have been going to this branding for so long, the Homms have a kind of priority in the roping pen; and some other people have jobs that only they do. It is traditional for youngsters and newcomers to mug before they rope. It is a kind of initiation. I mugged calves for about an hour, and then I got my turn at roping.

Cy recalls what happened next. "Colt, when your turn came to rope," said Cy, "I was taking a break. You went straight in and you were roping better than I had ever seen before."

I had been practicing a lot, so my rope flew true to help me keep my spot as a roper. But, of course, as soon as Cy mentioned it, I began to replay the scene in my mind. "You had just drug out a calf and were headed back to the pen when I called you over." Just thinking about what followed made Cy laugh so hard that he nearly couldn't continue with his story. "You rode to the fence, and I told you as seriously as I could to get down from your horse. You almost had your foot on the ground and with such a sad look on your face, I started to laugh. I told you then that if you don't quit roping so well, you are going to make me look bad."

Of course, it was all in the name of fun; although, I think Cy jinxed me when he said that because I didn't rope well the rest of the day. But my life is charmed, and I have been roping since my first branding when I was thirteen years old. One old hand told me that he was twenty-five years old before he had the chance to rope at a branding. Other people have never been able to rope; and here I am, eighteen years old and roping since I've been branding.

Toward the end of the day's regular branding, we had some yearling "herd bulls" to castrate and brand, so Cy had me get down to mug. This was so that none of the "guests," the less experienced people, got hurt. Also, situations like that demand people who work well together, as Bob and Cy and I do.

"I enjoy branding in the springtime," says Cy. "Everything is fresh and new, and the cattle and the horses work well. Everybody feels good and is excited to work."

Methods of Branding

Another method of branding uses a calf cradle. A calf cradle is basically a miniature squeeze chute. A calf gets pushed into it head-first and then is latched into the head gate. The crew then squeezes in the side of the chute and rolls the table so the calf is on its side. Once on its side, the crew has easy access to any part of the calf that needs tending. Cy has a strong opinion about calf cradles. He says, "Calf cradles should be outlawed. They are hard on the calves, a lot more work than dragging, and not near as much fun."

Personally, I agree. I have worked equal amounts of cattle both

Calf cradles such as this one, viewed from the front, snuggly and safely hold young calves for branding. Writing Lab photo.

ways, and the dragging proves much quicker. Roping does require more people, however. For a small herd or a place with only two or three people available, a cradle is handy. The least favorable aspect of using a cradle is that the calves have to be pushed into the cradle, and it gets very messy. (The calves "get the crap scared out of them," literally.) People also get kicked and stepped on a lot.

Roping and dragging also has its dangers, though. Horses, if not handled properly or if spooked for some reason, can run over people or buck off riders. In addition, hot irons sizzle dangerously, vaccine needles flash around, and sharp knives flutter daringly. Larger cattle are much stronger and can push and pull muggers around, and they could fall or step on people who are not careful. Mugging takes skill and, if not done just right, can lead to extra hard work.

But more people get seriously hurt when using the cradle, mostly in the form of broken toes, stepped-on feet, and very sore shins. Roping is also the original way.

The Cowboy's Horse

Bob Homm told me, "A man in a pen is nothing without the right horse. The calves are moving all around and often times under

Two of Cy Homm's blanketed ranch horses stay warm during their "off" time. Writing Lab photo.

the horse. He's got to have the right temperament. The horse needs to remain calm in the roping pen. Once you have a calf caught and you turn to ride out of the pen, your rope could go under the horse's tail or rub along his lower legs." This will cause many horses to "blow up." Calves struggle on the end of the rope, so the pressure changes on the saddle, and a slight pinch could put a horse into a spastic, raging fit. Also, as many people have found out the hard way, a lot of horses are not too keen on smoke. When the iron starts to scorch the hair on the calf, smoke rolls and the calf panics; this also puts strain on the rope and spooks many horses.

"You do not want too young of a horse in the pen," says Bob. "Immature horses~I mean the horse's body being immature~can hurt themselves. They can strain wrong and pull muscles or bones out of whack. It can ruin a good horse for pulling. As has been said many times, 'A cowboy is only as good as his horse.' If a horse won't pull, that doesn't mean he is not a good horse to have; but if you are in a position that needs a puller, you had better find the right horse."

A Cowboy's Life

Cy and Bob both cowboy for a living and their experiences provide enough information to fill volumes. But there is work to be done and miles to be ridden. Calves for the spring branding are being born right now, and I have been helping out at the Bar T through this calving season. It is exciting to know that those calves that I am pulling, and the ones I have to carry back to the barn when it is below zero weather with blizzard-like conditions, are the ones that we will be putting "the mark" on later. I fight the adverse conditions, angry mother cows, coyotes, and lack of sleep to do my job, just like every other cowboy. Being a cowboy requires all of these things and a love of the work. The stressful moments and hard work go into what I do; but seeing those calves born, branded, driven to grass, and weaned make it all worthwhile.

Atop the branding irons lies a set of old-time dehorning shears, used to cut horns off of cattle. Charles Lowel Baker, Colt's great-grandfather, handmade the spurs in the foreground. Writing Lab photo.

Smokin'

Colt Strick

Ropes and cattle
an old double rig saddle
The calves start to mill
The cowboy like some creature of prey
awaits his chance
with one daft move
snares two hind feet
quick now but fluid and steady
his hand flashes to the horn
slack coming tight he turns
toward the gate
one wrap then two
his dallies hold the rope
as he drags the calf to
the fire, a hot iron awaits
this li'l doggie
suffers his fate
a scorch mark upon his hide
shows he is owned
another possession
just as the ropes and cattle and
an old double rig saddle

My Cowboy's Poetry

His Freedom

Colt Strick

Not a gesture a country can offer
not a thing any person can give or take
but for the cowboy it's necessity
as important as his run-down boots
his big flash horse
like his dog
his best roping saddle
he couldn't go without it
Cowboy Freedom

Sources:
Cy Homm, Burlington, Colorado
Bob Homm, Burlington, Colorado
Time-Life Books editors and William H. Forbis. *The Old West: The Cowboys.*
    Alexandria, Virginia: Time-Life Books, 1973.

Acknowledgments

We offer our thanks:

To all who allowed themselves to be interviewed, often on tape, and to have their stories printed.

To all who freely handed over family heirloom photos and artifacts for us to use. We recognize the risk they took and appreciate their trust.

To those who gave time for a group interview and shared their knowledge one Saturday morning at the Prairie Vista Restaurant: Bob Wood, Burdine Homm and Clarence Lidke. And to all who telephoned us or wrote letters filled with information because they weren't able to attend.

To all who read our articles or stories prior to publication and checked the facts for assurance that what was written matched their knowledge and memories.

To our grant awarders, El Pomar Youth in Community Service and Service Learning Grants, for believing in our process and product enough to help fund it.

To SUNWEST bank for their generous donation to help with publishing costs.

To Dennis Schiel, Artist, for his input on photography and formating, but especially for his extreme patience in working with us on deadlines and for giving us room to change our minds.

To Dennis Schiel for permission to quote from *Idalia Centennial 1887-1987*, a news magazine he originally published but which is now out-of-print.

To the wonderful ladies at the Wray Museum, Linda-Marie Vermillion and June Redman, for openly and graciously sharing valuable information with us, and especially to June for the resource books she bought and donated to the Writing Lab.

To all individuals involved in *Gusts of Dust* in any way, but whom we haven't specifically named.

* * * * *

Corrections for Volume II:

The photo on page 24 is actually of Col. James D. Garcia, son of Doctor James Garcia.

Page 45 and *Yuma County Cemeteries* (our source) list "Ida and Ernest Nash Children" as buried at the Lucas Cemetery. Phyllis Weyerman, daughter of Ida and Earnest (with the a), believes the three undated graves may hold the children of some ancestors.